Contents

Contents

 # Introduction

Is this the Job for You?

☐ Do you like meeting people?

☐ Do you like helping people to solve their problems?

☐ Are you good at communicating with people?

☐ Are you prepared to take on responsibility?

☐ Can you keep a confidence?

☐ Can you cope with pressure?

☐ Do you seek to build a long-term career?

☐ Do you dislike desk work?

☐ Do you dislike convention?

☐ Do you want to move from job to job all over the world?

The more times you answer 'Yes' to the first seven questions, the more likely it is that a career in the law will suit you. But if you answer 'Yes' to the last three questions, the law may not be for you after all.

The law offers a wide variety of fascinating careers. Not everyone can become a judge or a magistrate, but in addition to barristers, advocates and solicitors, many people work in a range of jobs that keep the legal system running smoothly. There are plenty of opportunities for office staff as well as a growing number of posts which reflect the fact that the law today is a business as well as a profession.

Careers in the law are often rewarding in terms of job satisfaction as well as financially. Television series such as *Kavanagh QC* and *This Life*, as well as the novels written by solicitors such as Frances Fyfield (creator of Helen West, a Crown Prosecution solicitor) and myself (featuring the Liverpool lawyer and amateur detective Harry Devlin), have perhaps helped to persuade viewers and readers that legal life is far from dull. And in the real world, although the legal market place is increasingly competitive and sometimes highly pressured, by and large the law still offers a reasonable degree of job security to those who have the right skills and are prepared to work hard.

But it is important to realize that the law does not offer an easy route to riches: a survey which made front page news in *The Law Society's Gazette* in 1997 reported that although the number of former Legal Practice Course students still in debt had fallen to 64 per cent, the average level of their debt had risen to £7000. The average cost of completing the vocational stage of training was recently estimated at £10,000, taking into account living expenses. Fortunately, help is sometimes available.

Good qualifications are necessary for some careers in the law, but not for others. In any event, having certain personal qualities – especially integrity and discretion – is important in all areas of the profession. There are opportunities not only in solicitors' firms and at the Bar, but also in industry, in central and local government and the academic world. Pressure groups, charities and law centres also offer openings which many people find more fulfilling than those on offer in more traditional legal offices.

The legal system in England and Wales differs from those in Scotland and Northern Ireland and the rest of the world. This means that qualifications you gain in one of the UK jurisdictions may not readily help you to find work either in another part of the UK or abroad, although you may be able to re-train.

The law and the legal profession are currently undergoing a major transformation. Many of the old barriers, such as those between the work of solicitors and barristers, are breaking down. As this book went to press came the news that a new law degree course is to be run by the Open University in partnership with the College of Law, a move hailed by the Lord Chancellor as providing a wider variety of people of different ages and from different social and educational backgrounds with the chance to enter the profession.

The opportunities for women and for minority groups are steadily increasing, although full equality has not been achieved. A Trainee Solicitors Group 1997 survey revealed that white male trainees were paid, on average, £779 pa more than their female counterparts, while 50 per cent of ethnic minority trainees were on the then minimum salary, compared with 26 per cent of trainees as a whole. But awareness of discrimination has undoubtedly increased and that awareness should help to contribute to continued improvement, over time, in the statistics.

Lawyers are, of necessity, increasingly having to specialize in particular aspects of their subject. There is a marked tendency for solicitors' firms to become larger. Yet it is possible to buck the trend successfully. The Solicitors' Indemnity Fund reported in June 1997 that the remuneration of sole practitioners was rising at a faster rate than that of all other law firms.

This book deals with the present state of affairs, but anyone thinking of a legal career needs to have an eye to the future and to be aware that the nature of the jobs available continues to evolve. The factual information set out later is based on the latest data obtained at the time of writing, but it is worth bearing in mind that details are subject to constant change and it is always sensible to check the up-to-date position as regards any point of importance. A good deal of material, especially on becoming qualified and getting started, has been kindly supplied by the professional bodies themselves, and the care and attention that they are devoting to the provision of information to would-be lawyers are an encouraging sign for the future. I have much appreciated the help readily given by many of the bodies mentioned as sources of further information later in this book.

It is a truism that any job will only give you back as much as you are prepared to put into it. So it is for legal work. But whatever level you are at, you will find that there is scope to earn more and take on further responsibility and as a result to develop not only your career but, far more importantly, yourself.

2 The structure of the profession

The main employment opportunities in the law are to be found in:

◆ industry and commerce
◆ private law firms (usually partnerships of solicitors) or barristers' chambers
◆ central government
◆ local government
◆ other private and public sector employers
◆ voluntary organizations.

There are also opportunities to become self-employed. In particular, many barristers and advocates are self-employed.

Barristers, advocates and solicitors

A notable feature of the legal system of the UK is that there are two distinct branches of the legal profession. Lawyers are either solicitors or barristers in England and Wales and Northern Ireland, and solicitors or advocates in Scotland. These two branches are separate in their organization, working system and main functions, although there may be a considerable overlap in the nature of their work in individual cases. The training of the two branches is separate. You must choose to become either one or the other in one of the three jurisdictions and, although it is possible to move from one branch to another and from one jurisdiction to another, once you are qualified, it is unusual to do so.

If you are moving in either direction, or changing jurisdictions, you are usually required to undertake further exams or training.

The traditional view is that the relationship between a solicitor and a barrister or advocate is akin to that between a family doctor and a consultant in the medical profession. Solicitors take instructions direct from clients, whereas barristers and advocates are not allowed to deal direct with the public and all their work has to be referred to them by solicitors or (in certain cases) by members of specified professional bodies, such as the Institute of Taxation. However, the traditional view implies that all members of the Bar (as barristers and advocates are sometimes collectively called) are each individually more specialized in their area of work than the solicitors who refer work to them. This is not necessarily the case. In many firms of solicitors, while the organization as a whole undertakes a very broad range of work, the individual solicitors deal only with certain types of case (some may specialize in conveyancing, others in litigation) and while it is true that many barristers or advocates are specialists, a significant number, particularly in Scotland, have a very broad-based practice.

The main traditional difference between the two branches of the profession was that although solicitors could represent clients in the lower courts and before tribunals (for example, industrial tribunals), barristers or advocates had a 'right of audience' (the right to appear and speak on behalf of a client before a court) before all the courts in the jurisdiction in which they had qualified. It is still the case that, for the most part, a solicitor's day is organized around his or her office, whereas the barrister or advocate is normally involved in a far greater amount of court work. It should be noted, however, that solicitors now have wider rights of audience in the courts, and an increasing number of them will be taking up the option to practise in the higher courts.

Another significant difference between the two branches of the profession is that while solicitors can form partnerships in which the partners are self-employed persons, who can employ other solicitors and other staff, barristers or advocates cannot form partnerships. Barristers in England and Wales work from premises (known as 'chambers') with other barristers, but they remain in practice on their own. Barristers in Northern Ireland and advocates in Scotland do not rent premises in this way but work independently, from the Bar Library at the Royal Courts of Justice in Belfast and the Advocates' Library in Edinburgh respectively.

Judges

Judges do not come from a separate profession. In other countries they often form part of the public service and are trained specifically for the job, but in the UK they are appointed by the Crown mainly from among leading barristers or advocates, although some judges (particularly circuit judges) are selected from among the ranks of more senior solicitors.

Not all judges sit in formal court rooms, wearing wigs and robes. Recently there has been an increase in the number of tribunals which have, in effect, a judicial function, such as industrial tribunals and social security appeal tribunals. These often have lay members but the chairman of the tribunal is invariably a lawyer. Tribunals usually hear cases in less formal surroundings, and neither the tribunal members nor the barristers or advocates or solicitors appearing before them wear wigs or gowns.

It is perhaps worth mentioning that in England, Wales and Scotland, justices of the peace (commonly called 'magistrates'), who are the judges most people have dealings with, have no formal legal training at the time they are selected. Although in larger cities 'stipendiary' magistrates are selected from among experienced lawyers, most magistrates are laymen who receive training after their selection and hear cases with the aid of a legally qualified justices' clerk. There are no lay magistrates in Northern Ireland and all magistrates there are either solicitors or barristers of at least seven years' standing. They are called resident magistrates or RMs.

Women in the legal profession

Among judges, barristers, advocates and solicitors, men outnumber women, particularly at the higher levels. In the past, women have often had to choose between a career and children. However, there is an increasing number of women now qualifying in both branches of the profession and in all three jurisdictions. Currently, over half the students passing the solicitors' final examination in England and Wales are women. There is thus increasing pressure on the profession to react more flexibly than in the past to women's preferred career patterns.

Ethnic minorities in the legal profession

Traditionally, the number of members of ethnic minorities who worked within the legal profession was small. In particular, very few judges, solicitors or barristers came from ethnic minority backgrounds. The picture is now beginning to change. For example, the Law Society has set the solicitors' branch of the profession proposed employment targets in this area. It is suggested that firms with between six and ten fee earners should try to have one ethnic minority fee earner on the staff, while larger firms should aim for 5 per cent of fee earners and 10 per cent of their trainees to be from ethnic minorities.

Disabled persons in the legal profession

The Disability Discrimination Act 1995 is a landmark measure which gives disabled persons a range of significant new rights in terms of employment and access to goods and services. It applies to employment in the legal profession and should help to break down barriers. In addition, organizations such as the Group for Solicitors with Disabilities are helping to promote a positive image of people with disabilities within the profession and society as a whole.

3 The jobs

Solicitors

The demand for solicitors' skills has grown steadily over the years. The number of solicitors practising in England and Wales is now over 70,000. There are over 7600 solicitors in Scotland and about 1400 in Northern Ireland. In all three jurisdictions there has been a sharp increase in the number of admissions in recent years with also a marked increase in the number of women qualifying. Solicitors come from a range of social backgrounds and, although about 84 per cent of them are in private practice, others practise in commerce and industry, local and central government, the Crown Prosecution Service and in the Magistrates' Courts Service. It is possible for an able solicitor who possesses both the academic and personal skills required to find good, interesting and satisfying employment, although this varies depending upon the specialism practised and the state of the economy. Many solicitors have earnings comparable with those of other graduate professions, but the profession has – like many others – been affected by the impact of the recession and demand in some areas has reduced with commensurate loss of earnings and even redundancy in some cases.

The Law Society provides advice about qualifying as a solicitor and the opportunities available, including (for England and Wales) the concise and very useful leaflet *The Law Degree Route to Qualification as a Solicitor*, which has provided valuable source material for this book and is highly recommended. Brochures and information issued by the Law Society are available from most local authority, school and college career services. There are now also detailed requirements with regard to continuing education after one has been admitted to the Roll of solicitors. Again, details are available from the Law Society.

Working in private practice as a solicitor

It is worth considering well in advance what you would like to do when you have qualified as a solicitor. It may take from three to six months to find the sort of job you want in the type of firm you want to work in, so do not leave it too late.

Some trainees and apprentices are offered work by the firm they train with, but since most firms will have several trainees qualifying at the same time, you cannot count on this happening. Nor should you view the lack of such an offer as being a reflection on your abilities.

Those who move firms on qualifying have to start on the round of replying to advertisements and attending interviews. In England and Wales, legal periodicals and several newspapers carry advertisements for solicitors' jobs. In Scotland you should consult the *Journal of the Law Society of Scotland*, and also *The Scotsman* and *The Herald*. In Northern Ireland your starting point may well be the *Belfast Telegraph*, the *Belfast Newsletter*, the *Irish Times*, or local newspapers.

The Law Societies of England and Wales and Scotland have an appointments registry to which you can add your name and from which you can obtain the names of firms who have registered vacancies for qualified staff at all levels. In England, Wales and Northern Ireland there are also commercial agencies that match applicants to the jobs on their files. Their service is free to the employee but commission, which is related to the employee's salary, is charged to the firm once the employee has successfully served a probationary period (usually three months). Some firms rely heavily on agencies; others respond favourably to approaches made by applicants themselves.

Having been a trainee or apprentice you will have come into contact with a number of people in the profession: other trainees, barristers, advocates and their clerks, court clerks, etc. Don't forget your contacts when looking for a job. Tell people in the profession: they often hear of vacancies that might not otherwise be advertised. Later chapters deal with alternatives to private practice which you may find interesting.

Assistant solicitors are employees and, as such, have little or no control over the organization in which they work. Not all assistants want the responsibilities or ties of being a partner, and some remain assistants throughout their careers. This may occur more in the future, given the increase in the numbers qualifying.

Partnership

Private practices are sometimes run by sole practitioners, but are more often partnerships of solicitors. If you are offered a partnership it may be as an equity partner, that is a partner with a share in the capital of the firm who takes from the profits in proportion to his or her share. Particularly in larger firms, it is more usual these days to be offered initially a salaried partnership, whereby you are still paid a fixed salary and do not usually take part in any significant decision-making, but would be more involved than an assistant solicitor in the day-to-day administration of the firm.

Being a salaried partner is usually regarded as a stepping stone to a full partnership, allowing both parties a probationary period, since it is generally anticipated that when you become an equity partner you are making a commitment to the particular firm for the rest of your working life. That commitment is usually sealed by a capital contribution made by the new equity partner.

Occasionally, equity partnerships are offered which do not require the new partner to make any further contribution other than his or her continued efforts, but usually, if you want to be a full partner, you will have to be prepared to pay for the privilege. You may have to borrow money and it has been known for solicitors to earn less in the first few years as equity partners while they are repaying the loan than they did as salaried partners or assistants. Equity partners are, of course, self- employed.

Commitment to a partnership must be more than just a financial one. A partner in a small provincial firm has summed up the key issues:

> The most important things to ask yourself when you are offered a partnership are whether you trust those who would be your fellow partners and, second, whether you respect them for the work they do. You must like the geographical location of the firm, as you are going to be there a long time, and of course you've got to enjoy the type of work you'll be doing there. If those aspects of the deal are OK, you then go on to examine the financial proposals.

Where to work

The differences between city and country practices reflect, to some extent, the differences between large and small firms. But this is not always the case: towns sometimes boast relatively large commercial firms, and all cities have their 'family firms'. However, some people prefer to work in a small community, of which they can become a part, where they can be closer to clients and come to know them and their families socially. Country solicitors often establish closer co-operation with other professionals, such as doctors, social workers, bank managers and the police, and this can be helpful in achieving quick and efficient results for the client.

As a very broad generalization, the pressures of a country practice are less, if only because the working environment is more pleasant and work is more integrated with the rest of life. Some people may find working in the country too confining for their tastes, and certainly, whatever you do, it is difficult to remain anonymous. If you want to keep your options open, it is probably best to work in a city at first and move out to the country later.

The type of firm

When choosing a firm at any stage in your career you should think carefully about what sort of firm you want to join; large or small, specialized or general. Larger firms tend to be more departmentalized which means that solicitors working in them tend to be more specialized also. Specialization may appeal to you, and certainly it follows on from the academic background that many solicitors now have. Some, however, prefer their work to be dictated by the clients for whom they work, so that they deal with whatever problem the clients bring in. Large firms tend to be more bureaucratic but they can afford to provide employees with modern office equipment, extensive libraries, and additional back-up services that may prove necessary for cases that are too large for one person to manage without help. However, you might also find a large organization impersonal: it will take a long time to get to know everyone else in the firm, and unless you are a partner you will seldom be involved in the way the organization is run.

Medium-sized firms can have the best (or worst) of both worlds, allowing you to specialize while keeping a fairly broadly based case-load. In a medium-sized firm, each partner will tend to have his or her own clients who will dictate the type of work to be done. In a small firm there are none of the problems of getting to know all the other staff, and many solicitors enjoy feeling that their work contributes to the profitability of their firm. You may also find that, in fact, you are given great responsibility earlier in a small organization, because there are not a number of other assistants employed who are just as competent as you are.

Sometimes whole firms are specialized, and while they may provide an all-round service to their clients, their reputation is built on their work in one field in which the major part of their work is undertaken. Specialist firms come in all sizes and tend to be based in cities.

On the whole, salaries are lower in firms of two to four partners, and highest in firms of more than 20 partners. The size of a firm may, therefore, not only affect the type of work you do but also the amount of money you can expect to earn. The place where you practise is also relevant; earnings tend, naturally, to be higher in central London than in the provinces.

The type of job

Within private practice there is a great range of types of work you can do. Solicitors tend to be divided into those who undertake non-contentious cases, which do not involve any court work (conveyancing, both domestic and commercial; probate; trust work; company and commercial; tax) and those who deal exclusively with contentious or litigious matters, which result in court cases (matrimonial work; criminal and civil litigation). To some extent the sort of job you do will be dictated by your experience in articles, but you can change direction at that stage or later if you are sufficiently determined and can persuade an employer to give you the chance to branch out into a new field.

Case Study

Vincent *is a 41-year-old solicitor who has been qualified for five years, following two changes of career path.*

'I am a late arrival to the legal profession. I took my degree in languages and worked as a teacher for some years and as a translator in the Civil Service for a further six years. I was in my mid-thirties before I decided to try to qualify as a solicitor. I was successful in the CPE course and the Law Society Finals course and was offered employment as an assistant solicitor by the firm in which I trained.

After working for about 18 months exclusively on personal injury litigation, I gradually became more involved in the work of the firm's commercial department and I am now wholly engaged in that line of work. It is largely concerned with general business matters, such as formation of companies. I have been required on a number of occasions to "tailor-make" the company for the very specific requirements of the client. This will include drafting the Memorandum and Articles of Association and, in certain cases, where the company is seeking charitable status, ensuring that both the practical requirements of the client and the stringent legal requirements of the Charity Commission are complied with. There can often be a conflict between these two aspects and the ability to come up with a practical compromise acceptable to both client and the Charity Commission is necessary.

The drafting of contracts of employment, terms and conditions of sale of goods, business agreements and contracts forms a major element of my work. This aspect of legal work is perhaps most closely akin to my previous linguistic work and I have certainly found that the two disciplines are complementary.

The job is demanding and I will usually need to work for longer than the official hours of 9am – 5pm and sometimes at weekends. Time pressures can often be intense and many clients have high expectations as to the speed of service provided (particularly since the advent of the fax machine!).

All the work involves contact with people. It is obviously important that the advice that the solicitor gives is correct but it is just as important that the client understands why that advice is being given. It is the solicitor's job to guide the client through the procedures and also to explain them, ensuring that often complex matters are fully understood.

I have been able to make direct use of my languages to some extent in my work as a solicitor, and the teaching techniques which I acquired in my former job are often directly relevant when explaining a legal point to a client. I am pleased to say that any professional experiences and skills that I may have acquired before my change of career from linguist to lawyer have not been wasted.'

Barristers and advocates

The Bar

There are at present over 7000 practising barristers in England and Wales of whom over 1000 are women. The Faculty of Advocates in Scotland has 600 members of whom 350 are practising advocates, and there are over 350 practising barristers in Northern Ireland. Barristers or advocates are often referred to as counsel or collectively as the Bar. Their training and the organization of the profession vary in the three different jurisdictions, but the type of work they undertake is very similar. Most counsel are permitted to appear before the courts only in the jurisdiction in which they have trained, so, for example, if you train as an advocate in Scotland you would not normally appear in courts in England, Wales and Northern Ireland, although this is likely to become easier as a result of recent changes in the law.

What do barristers and advocates do?

The principal function of barristers and advocates is to appear in court and represent clients and plead their cases, although they also advise generally on legal problems. They cannot take instructions direct from members of the public, and they have all their work referred to them by solicitors (where litigation is involved), or other approved professions.

They are generally regarded as the specialist members of the legal profession, although some solicitors also become extremely specialized, and many members of the Bar maintain wide-ranging practices throughout their careers, being equally prepared to undertake criminal or commercial cases. Usually, solicitors help and advise the client from start to finish, and counsel are only called in to represent the client when the case comes to court.

Again this is a generalization, as solicitors can, and do, represent their clients in the lower courts. Equally, barristers and advocates may be asked to advise at relatively early stages in cases which may, in fact, never come to court, and some counsel, (for example, those involved predominantly in chancery work) make comparatively few court appearances.

However, the majority of barristers and advocates, as well as spending time drafting written opinions and pleadings and other documents necessary in the judicial process, also spend a considerable amount of time representing clients in court. Therefore, at the Bar you will have a rather different kind of working day from that of the average solicitor. All your researches, conferences and paperwork will have to be before and after court and, as most courts sit between 10am and 4.30pm, the working week for a barrister or advocate may consist of many early starts and late nights. However, you may not have enough work, particularly at the beginning of your career, and it is also difficult to cope with days when you have nothing to do.

Skills needed for the job

In all three jurisdictions, the job demands more from its practitioners than mere legal knowledge. A degree of physical and mental stamina is needed to keep up with the lifestyle and to withstand the pressures involved. You need to be determined to succeed and must be ambitious, as there has always been an element of healthy competition at the Bar.

To enable you to be in court most days, with a limited amount of time for preparation, you will have to develop an ability to assimilate facts quickly and also learn to be flexible enough to change from one job to the next with ease. You will also need to be able to think quickly on your feet. The exciting side of the job – the court appearances – hinges on mundane and thorough preparation, and to prepare well you will have to teach yourself to be painstakingly accurate.

Being self-employed

A factor to note, if you are considering a career at the Bar, is that barristers and advocates in practice are self-employed. Being self-employed has both advantages and disadvantages. Barristers and advocates are thus answerable only to themselves for the way they occupy their time, and they are able to assess directly the fruits of their labours. Theoretically, provided the work is available, an individual who wants more money simply works harder, and it is true to say that barristers and advocates, like solicitors, can earn more than most people. The corollary is that there is never a guaranteed income, and this can be a primary concern in the early years. Sometimes you will worry because you are too busy, sometimes because you are not busy enough. And even when the money is earned it may not be paid for a considerable time, sometimes for years. Yet right from the start, barristers and advocates have to pay all the expenses of running their own business. These include the costs of travelling to and from court; buying the correct clothes, including a wig and gown; buying books and periodicals; paying hotel bills if they are required to represent clients in other parts of the country; contributing to the running costs of the chambers from which they work; and paying a clerk.

Being self-employed, barristers and advocates usually need the services of accountants to help sort out their financial affairs and ensure that all the necessary returns, including VAT, are made. All expenses are tax-deductible but this is of little consolation when bills have to be paid far in advance of receiving any fees.

Working in private practice

In whichever jurisdiction you qualify when you start working in practice you will be referred to as a 'junior'. Some barristers and advocates remain juniors throughout their careers and the expression 'junior' is in no way a derogatory reflection on the individual's experience. However, some barristers or advocates decide after 10 or 15 years in practice to apply to be allowed to become a Queen's Counsel (QC), also called Leading Counsel or 'silks' in England and Wales, 'silks' and Senior Counsel in Northern Ireland, and Senior Counsel in Scotland. The application in England and Wales is made to the Lord Chancellor; in Scotland to the Lord Justice General; and in Northern Ireland to the Lord Chief Justice. Applications are considered on the basis of the applicant's proven ability during his or her career, bearing in mind the number of QCs already practising in the applicant's particular branch of the law. A balance has to be kept between the number of juniors and QCs working in different fields, as the nature of the work they undertake, and the fees they are paid, are different.

Having 'taken silk' (the expression arising from the fact that QCs are entitled to wear silk gowns), the QCs' fees are increased by about two-thirds and they become engaged principally in advising and court appearances. Junior counsel are usually engaged to assist QCs since barristers generally stop settling pleadings (that is, drafting the formal written statements which set out a party's case) after taking silk.

When a client goes to a QC, he or she is sure of obtaining the advice of an acknowledged expert in a particular branch of the law. Taking silk will help to confirm the reputation of a barrister or advocate, but the competition for work of the appropriate quality will be intense. Initially, because of the drop in the amount of work coming in, the QC may earn less than a busy junior.

The range of work for a barrister or advocate

As with solicitors, there is a wide range of work to choose from as a barrister or advocate. In Scotland, advocates tend to be less specialized and have to be prepared to deal with the very wide range of cases that are referred to them. This is also true of the practices of many barristers in England and Wales and Northern Ireland but, particularly in London, there are specialist chambers in which all the barristers are engaged almost exclusively in cases in one area of the law, such as chancery work or building cases or copyright matters. Barristers in specialist chambers often find it takes longer to build up a practice, but in the end the rewards can be greater. If you start work in criminal chambers, because there is a large amount of work available in that field it usually means that you will start to earn more at an earlier stage. As you are studying you should try to work out which areas of the law interest you in particular, and whether you are the sort of person who prefers to be in court every day dealing with a mixed bag of cases that might affect any individual, or whether you prefer to deal with large commercial matters which will involve you in research and bring you into contact with clients who are proba- bly quite well versed in their field.

The Bar in England and Wales

The Bar is, primarily, a self-regulating profession. The barristers' professional body is the General Council of the Bar, which gov- erns professional conduct and also looks after barristers' interests, for example in negotiating with the government over suitable rates of pay for publicly funded work. It is to some extent the 'voice' of the Bar and comprises elected barrister–members who are backed up by a full-time Secretariat.

The Inns

All barristers who intend to practise at the Bar of England and Wales have to be members of one of the four Inns of Court, which are in London. These are Lincoln's Inn, Middle Temple, Inner Temple and Gray's Inn. The Inns, which were originally more akin to colleges of law, serve several functions. Just as the three law societies are the only organizations that can admit stu- dents to practise as solicitors in the UK, so the Inns are the only societies that can 'call' students to the Bar in England and Wales to practise as barristers. In addition to providing the necessary authorization to practise, the Inns provide their members, both qualified and unqualified, with a basis for their professional and social life. Each Inn has a library where its members can work and a hall where they can lunch and meet, and there is a tradition of members dining together in hall on a regular basis to promote and maintain contact with each other. The Inns also have their own extensive buildings in central London which are let to barristers and other professional tenants as offices.

There are various levels of membership in the Inns, members being either students, barristers or Benchers. Benchers, or more properly, Masters of the Bench, are the senior members of the Inn, and are either practising or retired barristers or judges, who govern the Inns. They are co-opted by existing Benchers and each year one Bencher is chosen as Treasurer or administrative head of the Inn, though the day-to-day administrative work is carried out by the Sub- or Under-Treasurer and a permanent staff.

Chambers

Barristers, though self-employed, work from offices shared with other barristers, which are referred to as sets of chambers. If offered a vacancy in a set of chambers a qualified barrister becomes known as a Tenant. Tenants share the running costs of the chambers (such as rent, rates, heating and lighting expenses, stationery, telephone charges, and secretaries' wages). One barrister, usually the most senior, will hold the post of 'Head of Chambers' and it is usually with him or her that contracts for services (eg for the telephones, stationery and rent) are made on behalf of the chambers as a whole.

Barristers in chambers can provide each other with support both directly and indirectly. They can sometimes help each other by taking on work from one of their number who becomes too busy (a practice known as devilling in England and Wales; in Scotland the same expression is used to mean pupillage, see pages 74–8). They may lend books or the services of pupils and they can also support each other by discussing points of law or tactics, and more senior members of chambers can assist newcomers with problems of practice and etiquette. Sets of chambers are found in London and 32 other towns in England and Wales. The number of barristers in a set varies considerably from less than ten to more than 30.

The Bar in Scotland

All advocates in Scotland are members of the Faculty of Advocates. The principal officer of the Faculty is the Dean, who is assisted by other officers such as the Vice Dean, Treasurer, Clerk and Keeper. All these officers are elected annually and the Dean and the officers, together with the Faculty Council, constitute the governing body of the Faculty, controlling professional discipline and etiquette in much the same way as the Bar Council does in England and Wales.

Chambers in Scotland

In Scotland, advocates do not join together in sets of chambers as they do in England and Wales. An advocate can have as his or her chambers the Advocates' Library in Edinburgh, which is normally where advocates are to be found when they are not out of town, or they may have their chambers at home if they are within one mile of Edinburgh's Parliament House. In practice, almost everyone has chambers at Parliament House.

The Bar in Northern Ireland

Admission to the degree of Barrister-at-Law is the responsibility of the Honourable Society of the Inn of Court of Northern Ireland, of which all barristers are members. The government of the Inn is shared between the benchers of the Inn of Court of Northern Ireland, the Executive Council of the Inn of Court of Northern Ireland and members of the Inn assembled in general meeting.

Chambers

Barristers in Northern Ireland are self-employed but they do not join together in chambers or employ clerks as barristers do in England and Wales; rather, they practise from the Bar Library at the Royal Courts of Justice in Belfast. In that respect the Northern Ireland system is more akin to that of Scotland.

Case Study

Peter *is a barrister.*

'I started my pupillage in 1986 in chambers in a provincial city. Choosing to work outside London was not a conscious decision, but pupillages were in relatively short supply and, from what I could gather at the time, the chambers that made the offer had a good reputation. Today I am still there and I have not regretted my decision at all. I have now grown to realize that, for many people, working at the provincial Bar has considerable advantages over London (for example, living expenses) while still providing rewarding work and the opportunity to build up a substantial practice.

My work now is generally commercial, with an emphasis on sale of goods and consumer credit, but that was not always the case. During my first years in chambers, like all common law pupils, I did whatever work came my way. This included criminal and matrimonial cases, which now form no part of my practice. It is only when you have done different types of work that you can make a proper decision as to whether or not you wish to specialize and, if so, in which field. My advice to any prospective barrister would be to keep an open mind to start with and not aim for one given specialization from the outset. It would be no good deciding that you want to do crime all the time and then to discover that juries scare you rigid.

The type of work which I do now does not fall into the general public's common perception of a barrister's function. Many people, on hearing that I am a barrister, will ask me whether I prosecute or defend, when in reality I do neither. Instead, I spend many days working from home doing paperwork. That means drafting pleadings (the formal court documents which set out each party's case) or writing opinions to enable clients to assess their chances of success in a case, or what further preparation is needed before a case is ready for trial. I do nearly all of my work on a personal computer. Those days when I am in court may consist of an application before a District Judge which will last maybe an hour. For me, a fully contested trial is the exception rather than the rule.

It would be a foolhardy person indeed who is not nervous just before his or her first case. But after a few weeks' practising I had gained considerably in confidence and started to enjoy appearing in court and dealing with 'real cases' for 'real people'. After about six months I was receiving sufficient fees to enable me to support myself financially. After about six years I am thoroughly happy at the Bar and cannot imagine doing any other job.

As the Bar moves towards a more modern outlook and starts to understand that it is there to offer a public service rather than to exist in its own right, there is an increasing opportunity for practitioners to develop a practice which suits them rather than having to adopt preconceived notions about what a barrister should do and how he or she ought to behave. If you are considering the Bar as a career, spend time in different sets of chambers while you are still at university or college if you can. This will give you an idea of the different types of work that barristers do.'

Coroners

Coroners in England and Wales are appointed by local government, and those who are qualified to apply for appointment are barristers, solicitors or legally qualified doctors of five years' standing. In addition to the coroners who serve a local community, all High Court judges are automatically made coroners for the whole of the country.

The job of the coroner is to inquire into deaths occurring within the area in which he or she serves, where the deceased is known to have died violently, unnaturally, in prison or unexpectedly, or where the cause of death is unknown. A coroner can order a post mortem examination and, where necessary, an inquest. Inquests are held in the coroner's court, which considers the evidence concerning the cause of death.

In Scotland the job of the coroner is undertaken by Procurators Fiscal. In Northern Ireland coroners must be practising barristers or solicitors of not less than five years' standing.

Licensed conveyancers

The profession of licensed conveyancers was created in England and Wales as recently as 11 May 1987. Licensed conveyancers are men and women who are legally qualified to advise on all aspects of the transfer of rights to land and property. A degree is not required; every would-be licensed conveyancer applies for registration as a student with the Council for Licensed Conveyancers. The basic educational requirement is four GCSEs or equivalent including English, but mature students may be accepted on the basis of their experience alone.

Having registered, a student must pass the Council's examinations and fulfil a practical training requirement. Part I of the examination is of A level standard. Part II deals with areas of law, practice and accounting which are relevant to conveyancing. Exams are held twice a year. Most students attend part-time courses run at colleges throughout the country. Correspondence courses are also available.

Legal executives and paralegals

Solicitors throughout the UK have traditionally employed non-admitted personnel to assist them with their legal work. Today most firms in England and Wales employ non-admitted staff – often described as 'paralegals', a rather vague and ill-defined general term sometimes associated with former office secretaries who have developed a wider range of legal skills – to help with legal work. Estimates vary, but at present there are thought to be over 25,000 fee-earning paralegals (and possibly many more than that) working in private practice. The Institute of Paralegal Training, which incorporates the Association of Legal Secretaries, provides information on career possibilities for secretaries. In Northern Ireland non-qualified legal assistants are called law clerks, but their numbers are steadily dwindling and work which was traditionally undertaken by law clerks in Northern Ireland is now more often undertaken by trainees and qualified assistant solicitors, and in Scotland the pattern is similar.

In all three jurisdictions it is possible to join a solicitors' firm straight from school without any specific qualifications and start work as a clerk, learning the job from experience and informal tuition given in the course of employment by the solicitor employer. However, the Institute of Legal Executives was set up in England and Wales with the support of the Law Society in 1963, and this provides a recognized system of formal training and exams for such employment. The Institute also attempts to protect the status and interests of its members while improving the quality of recruits. The Institute currently has some 22,000 members, most of whom are in England and Wales, but some law clerks in Northern Ireland are also members, having prepared for the exam by correspondence course made available by its teaching wing, Ilex Tutorial Services Ltd.

Strictly speaking, the title 'legal executive' should only be applied to Fellows of the Institute (the Law Society only permits Fellows to be referred to as 'legal executives' in solicitors' publicity material and on their letter heading), but the expression has come to be used much more generally in colloquial usage. If you are keen on a legal career but do not feel you can undertake the solicitors' training, this alternative may well suit you. Once you are qualified as a legal executive, it is always open to you to take advantage of the exemptions given by the Law Society and go on to become a solicitor.

Once you have qualified as a Member, provided you are aged 25 or over and have completed five years in qualifying employment, including two consecutive years as a qualified Member, it is possible to apply for admission as a Fellow. Applications for enrolment as a Fellow have to be supported by a certificate of fitness signed by a partner or senior solicitor of the practice or department in which the applicant is employed. Once admitted as such, Fellows are entitled to use after their names the letters FInstLEx.

Whether a Fellow of the Institute or otherwise, there will always be a limit on what you can do independently. You will not have such an extensive right to represent clients in court as solicitors have, and you will not be able to set up in practice on your own, or become a partner in a firm.

With the increase in the number of solicitors qualifying, some firms may tend to employ young solicitors rather than legal executives or paralegals. However, many firms in England and Wales prefer to employ non-solicitors for certain types of work, since the fact that they tend to specialize means they develop a very useful in-depth knowledge of their own area of the law. In addition, firms may realistically expect that paralegals will be cheaper to employ and will stay longer in one job as there is not the pressure on them to move to find partnership prospects.

Although as a legal executive or paralegal you will always be working for a solicitor, more experienced clerks work with a minimum of supervision, and handle their own cases. They sometimes manage their own departments, and they have contact with clients in just the same way as solicitors do. Obviously, those who qualify as Fellows of the Institute are likely to hold more senior positions and have much less need of supervision.

Case Study

William is a 40-year-old legal executive who works in a medium-sized urban practice, specializing in property work.

'I went to work in a solicitor's office some 20-odd years ago, upon leaving school. At the time the opportunity to work in a solicitor's office appeared considerably more interesting, in the long term, than anything which could be suggested by my careers master at school.

The firm of solicitors which employed me was an old-established firm which mostly dealt with conveyancing and trust work. Initially, I was employed as an office boy but with the assistance and patience of the partners and staff, I obtained a good grounding in the day-to-day running of the firm and the various aspects of their work. I also attended evening classes on a Legal Executive course.

I rose within the ranks of the firm and because of the firm's background, I took a liking to conveyancing, in which I have specialized ever since.

Approximately ten years ago my firm amalgamated with a larger firm, for which I still work. In the main, I have enjoyed my work over the years and it can on many occasions be something of a challenge. I have had an interesting and varied work load dealing with all aspects of conveyancing and differing types of client from the first-time buyer who looks to you for guidance, to the commercial client who, if the truth be known, may well know more about the law than you do (or at least believes he does).'

Barristers' and advocates' clerks in England and Wales

Barristers' clerks in England and Wales constitute a small profession which is almost unknown outside the legal world. They are responsible for the administration of barristers' chambers and for the professional lives of the barristers they serve. The title 'clerk' is now a misnomer, since it does not adequately describe the managerial nature of the role. Possibly 'Chambers Manager' would today be a more accurate title for a clerk to chambers.

Each set of chambers has its own individual administrative organization but they all follow a broadly similar pattern. There is a senior clerk, known as the 'clerk to chambers' who is assisted by the first junior clerk, who acts as his deputy, and by other junior clerks and typists who are employed by the head of chambers, a senior barrister.

Most barristers' clerks start work in a set of chambers straight from school, as this is very much a profession where you start at the bottom and learn on the job as you move up. Although the pay is not at first exceptional, the profession provides opportunities for those who prove themselves able to make the grade to obtain considerable financial rewards and job satisfaction. A few applicants may have contacts in the field, but the majority will have heard of the job for the first time through local careers offices.

The basic educational requirements for a prospective clerk are four GCSEs at grades A to C, two of which must be English and mathematics. Equivalent qualifications may be accepted.

The job of a barrister's clerk

The barristers' clerk has to organize the barristers' day. This includes: accepting instructions from solicitors; ensuring that written advice given by barristers is typed and returned to instructing solicitors; arranging conferences for solicitors and their clients with counsel and making sure that any papers the barrister will have to see before advising are received in time for them to be read; checking the lists produced by the various courts to see whether the barristers in their chambers are involved in any cases listed for hearing, and then notifying the barristers and in certain cases the solicitors concerned. An important aspect of the work is that the clerk should establish trust and goodwill with court officials and the job requires a very high standard of integrity.

Sometimes a barrister will be briefed to appear in two cases that clash and, when that happens, the clerk tries to ensure, if the solicitors so require, that another barrister in the chambers can appear instead. A clerk's day is dictated to a large degree by the fact that the courts do not publish lists of the cases to be heard on one day until late afternoon of the previous day, and so it is only towards the end of a day that the clerks can find out where the barristers in their chambers will be appearing the next day and sort out any problems arising. Clerks also have to be available at lunch-times so that the barristers who are at court can ring in, either to take messages or to check their appointments. Thus, to succeed as a barristers' clerk you will have to be able to cope with demands being made on you by solicitors and time limits, as well as by the barristers themselves. Whatever the problems, clerks have to remain courteous – they are the public relations officers for the chambers, and the extent to which solicitors consider they get a good service from the chambers (which depends largely on their relationship with the clerk) may well affect the amount of work they send. To do this job you must be able to work under pressure and be prepared to work long hours and accept responsibility, but the quality most necessary, according to the Institute of Barristers' Clerks, is common sense.

Prospects

As a school-leaver starting work in chambers you will find you are expected to fill in where needed, however mundane the tasks.

Along with accompanying barristers to court and carrying their books and robes from one court to another, you will be expected to run errands, collecting and delivering papers, answering phones and making tea. For the first couple of years you must expect to be something of a general dogsbody, but as you gain experience and learn about the organization of the office and the legal system, you will be given specific areas of responsibility to relieve the more senior clerks. You will take over the responsibility of checking the court lists; you will start to accept instructions from solicitors and negotiate fees on behalf of the barristers; you may, as a more experienced junior clerk in chambers, have the job of writing up the diary showing where each barrister is to be on the following day.

It should be stressed that the profession of clerk, like that of barrister, although once an exclusively male domain, has become open to women and there are both senior and junior female clerks.

There are at present about 350 barristers' senior clerks and approximately 550 junior clerks. A junior clerk may have to move from one set of chambers to another to gain promotion and experience. When you become a senior clerk your responsibilities will grow. A senior clerk will be responsible for all members of chambers, while often nurturing the new entrants until they have established a practice of their own. In addition, the senior clerk is also the office manager, welfare officer and father-confessor rolled into one, to both staff and barristers alike. He or she has to make sure, for example, that the building is kept in good repair and that there are adequate funds for the bills to be paid.

Case Study

John is a senior clerk in chambers.

'The job has changed greatly since I started as a second junior in the Temple 30 years ago, to what is now in most cases the equivalent of a senior manager if not director in a multi-million pound business. I started my own career in an average sized set of common law chambers in the Temple, moving on after almost four years in that post to take a first junior clerk's position in divorce and probate specialist chambers. After a year in those chambers I was offered and took a junior clerk's position in a London-based circuit chambers operating on the North Eastern Circuit which meant moving to Leeds and working out of the various barristers' clerks' rooms that were within the court buildings of the Assize and Sessions towns throughout the circuit and of course from home. As most of our chambers' work came from local solicitors, we decided to open branch chambers in Leeds to provide a permanent postal address, manned telephone and to offer our clients better facilities for conferences and the like. I moved over ten years ago to take over as senior clerk to my present chambers.'

As can be seen from this case study, a career can be forged outside London but the opportunities for movement from job to job are limited by the small number of chambers in any provincial centre and a willingness to move home with all that entails may be required for advancement.

Clerks in Scotland

In Scotland, advocates do not join together in chambers as they do in England and Wales, but work from the Advocates' Library instead. The Bar in Scotland is divided into ten 'stables', each of which is served by an advocates' clerk and a deputy clerk employed by Faculty Services Ltd. The ten clerks as a group are directly supported by ten deputies, who are backed up by clerical and secretarial staff. Faculty Services Ltd employs accounting staff who deal with the issue and collection of the advocates' fees. There is also a typing pool available to deal with the output of the advocates, though a number of them also employ personal secretaries.

The number of advocates' clerks is too small to warrant a formal training programme and training is provided in-service. There are no formal educational standards that have to be established to apply for the job of a clerk, though clearly this is a matter which is taken into consideration when applications are under review.

The number of vacancies for clerks are relatively few since the clerks constitute a very settled workforce and recruitment has only been necessary to cater for the increasing number of practising advocates.

The job of advocates' clerk is very similar to that of the barristers' clerk in England and Wales. The clerk is an intermediary between instructing solicitors and counsel, and his or her responsibility is to ensure that the advocates within the stable receive an appropriate flow of work, and to advise solicitors which counsel are suitable and available for any particular case.

It should be added, however, that solicitors often send instructions direct to advocates without using the clerk as an intermediary. As in the case of barristers in England and Wales, advocates in Scotland contribute a proportion of their gross earnings towards the payment of their clerks but in Scotland the advocates pay Faculty Services Ltd which then pays the employed clerks. Advocates' clerks enjoy a progressive salary scale which is reviewed annually.

Clerks in Northern Ireland

Barristers in Northern Ireland work from the Bar Library of the Royal Courts of Justice, where each has a desk. They do not employ clerks either individually or collectively.

Court reporters

Court reporters, also known as shorthand writers, attend court hearings and take a complete verbatim record of the evidence, the judgments, the summings up and sometimes the speeches of counsel. They should not be confused with reporting barristers, who write reports of cases for legal journals, or with newspaper reporters who write summaries of hearings for the national press.

A record of court proceedings has to be made for two reasons. A case may be appealed and the appeal court will need an accurate account of the earlier hearing to see how the lower court reached its decision. In addition, as longer cases progress, the lawyers involved often wish to see a transcript of the day's proceedings, to remind them of the evidence that has been given and to help them prepare for the next stage of the case.

Court reporters in England and Wales

In most instances in the High Court and the Crown Courts, where the major civil and criminal cases are heard, an official record has to be made of the evidence given by witnesses and of the judge's summing up and the judgment. The Lord Chancellor appoints firms to undertake this duty, and their staff – the court reporters – take a note of the proceedings. Sometimes, court reporters will use a portable tape recorder to assist them, and some courts have installed tape recorders as the sole method of taking the record. It is the court reporter's job to produce any typed transcripts which may be required.

Firms which undertake court reporting are also sometimes called on to provide shorthand writers to take notes for conferences and meetings, both public and private, so while you may train and be employed primarily for working within the court system, your skills may involve you in other fields from time to time.

There are no formal educational requirements for joining the profession, but preference is given to those with GCSE and A level passes and shorthand speed of 150 words per minute. What you will need, if you are to make the grade, is an ability to type and take shorthand both quickly and accurately, and a sound knowledge of English. You will have to understand fully what is being said, even if the matters are technical or the evidence is given ungrammatically, so that you can take clear notes and produce a transcript which is grammatically correct, easily understandable and retains the original sense of what was said.

Verbatim reporting has undergone much change in recent years with the advent of computerized shorthand machines and Computer Aided Transcription (CAT). It is now possible to provide a facility for the deaf or hearing-impaired to follow court proceedings, by linking an electronic input machine to a television screen.

Most court reporters work on a freelance basis, and firms often engage self-employed court reporters. The income you make is likely to be much the same, whether you are employed or self-employed.

Court reporters have to be prepared to reach and maintain high standards in their work, and also to work irregular hours as required. Those who qualify usually find the job interesting and satisfying. You are not confined to an office, and although the same skills are always employed, no two cases are ever the same. You might spend three days recording a very technical commercial dispute, and then a week taking notes in a serious burglary case – you can never tell in advance.

Useful fact sheets are available from the British Institute of Verbatim Reporters (see Useful addresses), which incorporates the former Institute of Shorthand Writers and the National Society of Stenotypists. It seeks to promote the more efficient practice of the art of shorthand writing in legal and other proceedings and the raising of qualifications and status of its members. It encourages and maintains training and examination facilities for machine and pen verbatim reporters.

Court reporters in Scotland and Northern Ireland

Court reporters in Scotland are engaged when and where required from local firms of shorthand writers who specialize in this type of work. Shorthand writers are employed in the criminal courts in Northern Ireland for the trials of more serious crimes only, and computer-aided transcription is now used extensively. Civil proceedings in the High Court are tape-recorded and transcribed, when notice of appeal is lodged, by members of the Supreme Court typing pool.

Law costs draftsmen

The work of a solicitor has to be charged for, and, although many solicitors process their own bills, there are often instances when they rely upon law costs draftsmen to prepare formal bills for them. Large firms in particular will often count a law costs drafting facility as an important and integral part of their management structure. Unlike accountants or cashiers, law costs draftsmen combine a basic mathematical skill with a knowledge of the laws and procedures which apply to solicitors' costs and act as advisors to both the solicitor and the client on the subject of legal fees and associated matters.

The subject of how a solicitor charges for the efforts he or she undertakes on behalf of the client is governed by a minefield of rules and regulations in a manner quite unlike any other profession and where the type of work undertaken by the solicitor, whether it is 'contentious' business, ie when a solicitor acts for a client in court proceedings, including matrimonial disputes – or 'non-contentious' business, ie when a solicitor acts in an advisory or representative capacity, such as in the buying and selling of property or the winding-up of a deceased's estate, will have a significant bearing upon how the solicitor's remuneration is calculated.

Furthermore, while a client is generally liable for all the solicitor's charges, nevertheless there are instances where part of those costs are to be met either by another party or from a fund, or may be payable out of a public fund (as in the case of Legal Aid). The drawing of bills of costs in these latter instances in particular requires specialist technical knowledge. Thus, the application of an expertise in the field of law costs when preparing an account of solicitor's charges can be essential if the interests of both the solicitor and the client are to be properly protected.

Law costs draftsmen operate either 'in-house' as employees of a firm of solicitors or as freelance agents acting for any number of different firms. The tendency appears to be for the larger firms of solicitors to have their own costs department while smaller firms, with less of a demand for a full-time law costs drafting facility, will use independent law costs draftsmen, many of whom operate in association with other law costs draftsmen.

The work of a law costs draftsman

A law costs draftsman's work is varied and is not always restricted to the preparation of bills of costs. Security for costs, often sought at an early stage in an action, or quantum of costs as an item of damages are examples of areas where a law costs draftsman's expert advice might result in a valuable saving in time and expense.

The first task for the law cost draftsman is to sort out the file and papers and examine the action which the solicitor has taken on behalf of the client, examine who has done the work (whether it was a partner, assistant solicitor, legal executive or trainee) and how long it took. The law costs draftsman also sees what expenses the solicitor has incurred in the way of, for example, court fees or barrister's fees.

Having established what work has been done, the law costs draftsman has to apply the appropriate scale of charges in that particular court, prepare to support the level of fee earner employed (for example, examine whether it was a case which warranted the attention of a partner whose charge will be higher than a more junior fee earner) and prepare a case to justify the amount of time engaged, so far as such time can be claimed as directly attributable to the case in question, for example examine time spent which might have been avoided had the client given clearer instructions.

Once the bill is drawn, these and other factors may be put to the test in court proceedings called 'taxation' which takes place before an adjudicating officer called a Taxing Officer (who, in the County Court, will be a District Judge) and where the law costs draftsman will support the claim for costs against an adversary, probably another law costs draftsman whose job it will be, on behalf of the paying party, to apply legitimate arguments which will achieve as large a reduction in the bill as possible. The Taxing Officer, having read the papers and heard the arguments, will decide the proper level of fees and disbursements to be allowed.

Taxation is an adversarial process where the result can depend not only upon the strength of the arguments at the law costs draftsman's disposal but also the ability of the law costs draftsman to explain and put across those arguments to the Taxing Officer to the best effect.

The Association of Law Costs Draftsmen

As the average size of a solicitors' practice has grown, so the legal profession has become ever more cost-conscious. Attempts by solicitors to simplify billing by the introduction of computerized time recording systems has, in many instances, led to an increase in the number of disputes with clients over the size of bills. Furthermore, so far as costs recoverable from another party are concerned, such computer systems do not impress the courts, who will still require a solicitor's charges to be properly explained and for factors other than time to be given proper consideration. Different courts have different scales and procedures, and with the recent introduction of fixed rates for certain types of work, a law costs draftsman's skills are now in even greater demand.

In 1977 a number of eminent law costs draftsmen, concerned to maintain the standards which they considered were befitting such a branch of the legal profession, joined together to form the Association of Law Costs Draftsmen. This Association operates in England and Wales and boasts a membership in excess of 500, with a growing overseas contingent from the many countries around the world where the principles that operate in this jurisdiction are embodied in their own rules.

Membership of the Association is open to persons of good general education who are of employment age and are actively engaged predominantly in a career of law costs drafting. The Association aims to promote the status of the profession and maintain the standards of its membership. Students of the Association are encouraged to study and take the Association's examinations. Regular publications keep the membership abreast of changes in the law and seminars and workshops are regularly organized.

As awareness of the importance to the legal profession of able and experienced law costs draftsmen grows, employers are increasingly interested only in employing law costs draftsmen who have the advantage of membership of this Association.

Court workers

The smooth running of the day-to-day business of the courts throughout the UK is maintained by court administrators and clerical staff. There are many different jobs at various grades, some of which you can enter straight from school and others which require previous training, but they are all responsible jobs in which you will be encouraged to use your initiative.

Jobs in the courts are open to men and women, and to both school-leavers and more mature applicants alike. A career with the court service is secure, and what attracts most people are the possibilities for career development rather than financial incentives. Promotion is generally made from lower grades, which allows beginners to move up through the service as they gain experience, and training is often made available.

Jobs in the Magistrates' Courts

Initial enquiries about careers in magistrates' courts should be referred to the Magistrates' Courts Division of the Lord Chancellor's Department. Clerical and administrative work is undertaken in magistrates' courts by justices' clerks' assistants. They are not civil servants, but none the less enjoy a secure living and pension rights similar to their colleagues in other courts.

To work in a magistrates' court you may need GCSE English or its equivalent, but many applicants, in fact, have A–levels or degrees. Training in office and administrative procedure and elementary law is given to beginners, and there are courses provided as you gain experience.

The Lord Chancellor's Department can offer a varied and interesting career connected with the law. Entry is usually at one of three main levels: Administrative Assistant, Administrative Officer or Executive Officer. The type of work will depend substantially upon the grade at which staff are employed. The following gives an indication of what can be expected.

Administrative Assistant

This is the first rung of the administrative staff ladder. The duties tend to be routine and typically involve keeping records, sorting and filing papers, and some simple figure-work, perhaps using a calculator. There may be some straightforward letter-writing and time spent dealing with enquiries from the public. The job is very much like that of a junior clerk in a large business firm, with neatness and accuracy as the prime virtues. There is no typing – that is a separate job – but Administrative Assistants in some offices may be employed on other kinds of keyboard operation. The grade has no supervisory role and is supervised by the Executive Officer.

Administrative Officer

This is the main clerical grade in the Civil Service. The duties call for the exercise of discretion and initiative within set guidelines. Administrative Officers handle incoming correspondence; they write or draft letters; they give all kinds of advice and assistance to the public, either over the telephone or across the counter; they assess fees and payments, and they check accounts and keep statistics and various records. They sometimes work with Administrative Assistants but they are given – and are expected to accept – more responsibility. Many Administrative Officer posts in the Lord Chancellor's Department are in areas which are subject to heavy workload pressures, such as in the 300 or so County Courts where speed and reliability are among the essential qualities.

Executive Officer

The Executive Officer grade is the first level in the administration group of Civil Service grades in which the management and supervision of staff are likely to constitute a significant part of the work. In a County Court, an Executive Officer could expect to head a small team of Administrative Assistants or Officers and would be responsible for organizing them and their work. He or she would also deal with complex or difficult situations which the administrative staff could not be expected to handle, for example the problems posed by particularly angry or distressed members of the public. By contrast, a new Executive Officer in a Crown Court would not normally have a staff management responsibility but would start work as a Court Clerk, sitting in court with the Judge and swearing in the jury, taking the defendant's plea, keeping a brief note of the proceedings and assessing the fees claimed by the barristers. After about a year as a Court Clerk, he or she might then move on to another area of Crown Court work (for example, the listing of court cases) which might involve an element of staff supervision.

About 50 per cent of Executive Officer posts are in the County Courts and 10 per cent in the Crown Courts, but there are also opportunities outside these areas, for example in the Department's headquarters in London (personnel, finance, accommodation, training, etc), in the High Court in the Royal Courts of Justice, or in a number of associated offices and tribunals.

Practice manager

Increasingly, large firms of solicitors (and also some barristers' chambers) are finding that they need the administrative skills of a practice manager. Like company secretaries in industry, the functions of practice managers vary in different organizations, but they are usually individuals with either company secretarial or accountancy qualifications. An ability to manage computerized accounting systems will be an asset. Practice managers have high-status jobs which often pay high salaries. In small firms the functions of a partnership secretary are usually undertaken by one of the partners, assisted by the firm's accountant.

Case Study

Ian is practice manager of a provincial solicitors' firm.

'I am by training an accountant. When I was at Polytechnic, I did a foundation course for the examinations for the Institute of Chartered Accountants. I then took up a training contract with a firm of accountants and passed the foundation course and the first part of my professional examinations. At that point, however, I decided on a change of tack and, instead of proceeding with further examinations with a view to qualifying as an accountant, I moved into industry as a Company Secretary with an engineering business. I then joined a family-owned wholesaling company as the in-house accountant. I progressed within that company and eventually became Finance Director. I stayed with the business for 11 years until trading difficulties prompted me to seek a change of direction.

At that point, a recruitment agency asked me if I would be interested in being interviewed for a position as practice manager of a solicitors' firm. I did not know what the post entailed and was, initially, uncertain about it. However, the firm in question was one with which I had had dealings during my time in industry and I made up my mind to join. I found that there were not as many financial controls in place as I would have expected. One of my initial tasks, therefore, was to try to put appropriate financial systems in place. Another important requirement was to take on a problem-solving role and use my experience of industry to help the partners guide the firm through a period of growth and transition. I often acted as a channel of communication between the partners and the staff, especially in the firm's branch offices.

As the initial tasks have been completed, my role has changed somewhat. It is now very similar to the role of a Finance Director in industry. I find that my previous experience in business is very useful, not least because it has given me some insight into the 'real world'; some people within professional firms (accountants as well as solicitors) perhaps lack the necessary ruthlessness to get the best deals from suppliers (including, for example, computer suppliers, insurance brokers and suppliers of consumables). Learning to cope with the specialized rules in relation to solicitors' accounts was something of a culture shock to begin with. That apart, however, the financial disciplines within a solicitors' firm are much the same as in any other well-run business. I am involved with the preparation of annual accounts, budgets and financial forecasting. The environment in which I now work may be totally different from that of my previous employers, but the goal is exactly the same – to run the business profitably.'

Legal secretaries

Legal secretaries, like solicitors, tend to specialize in particular areas of the law. You will probably find that you will gain experience in one field, say, conveyancing and then be even more valuable in the eyes of a prospective employer, who will know that you can be left not only to type what is dictated accurately and in the correct format, but you will also recognize the right forms to use and fill them in with a minimum of explanations. You will know when to take copies, when to provide enclosures and what to tell clients who ring up to find out how their cases are progressing. Some firms allow experienced secretaries in conveyancing departments to attend completions, or experienced secretaries in litigation departments to attend court to take notes of the proceedings.

Many people considering legal secretarial work think that they will be personal assistants to their bosses, but in the past there were relatively few openings of this kind. One of the reasons for this was that solicitors tend to use trainee solicitors to do some of their administrative chores, since their training consists of learning office practice as well as law. In addition, the almost universal use of audio machines means that secretaries spend little time taking dictation from their bosses and are therefore less likely to become involved in the cases, beyond typing the correspondence and documents. Very often legal secretaries find that they are kept busy typing and developing other technical skills, such as operating computer systems, rather than becoming directly involved in the cases and having very much contact with clients.

However, there are legal personal assistant jobs around and if that is what you have in mind, one course is to follow up the advertisements that specifically ask for PAs. It is also worth bearing in mind that a number of secretaries do become skilled lawyers, whether as paralegals, legal executives or (ultimately, and in practice in a very small minority of cases) solicitors. The Institute of Paralegal Training publishes a useful leaflet called *Becoming A Legal Secretary* (see Useful addresses).

Temporary Work

Some legal secretaries prefer to do temporary work. Temps are employed by agencies who hire out their services to firms who become short-staffed or over-worked for a while. The firms pay the agencies on an hourly rate and the agencies pay the secretaries. Usually, temporary work pays better than a permanent job, but the real benefit is that you get as much flexibility as you can afford. You are paid for the hours you work, and if you want a day off you just inform the agency in advance. Of course, when there is less work about you run the risk of not being able to work as long as you might wish to, but many people prefer to run that risk in order to be able to organize their days to suit themselves, or to fit in with family commitments. It can also be exciting to go to different offices – you get changes of scene and meet many more people. You also get wide-ranging experience in office procedures (which differ from firm to firm) and real self-confidence from knowing you are good enough at your job to be able to just walk in and pick up the threads.

Case Study

Ann *is a secretary in a large city centre solicitors' office, where she has worked for more than 15 years.*

To earn a living as a legal secretary is not as stultifying as it might first appear, although typing one's way through the intricacies of a local search is only marginally more interesting than typing out bills of lading or shipping manifests. There are rich seams of human interest to be tapped in all facets of legal work, from the outwardly dull house-purchasing aspects, via the joustings of the Family Division in divorce work to the quieter world of wills and probate. These are just three areas of law that can be covered in the capacity of a legal secretary.

There are other newer areas such as industrial relations where the tribunals and ACAS hold sway; high-powered mergers in company law involving huge amounts of cash, to problems involving EU law or the environment. There are aspects of criminal law, for example, cases involving child neglect, incest or even murder. It is all there, every aspect of humanity, its failings and its strivings.

Your job as a secretary is, in effect, to grease the wheels, to keep the moving parts moving. You will type letters, operate word processors, liaise with computers, make appointments and make tea – sometimes lots of it. As you become proficient in dealing with matters and handling clients there are always opportunities to advance in the clerical side of the office, perhaps accounts or possibly into paralegal work. The 'in at the deep end' experience gained from being a legal secretary has been an extremely useful launch pad for many other careers in the legal profession.

Each firm of solicitors is different – each branch of each firm is different. The pecking order and status quo of each office are different.

But the job of legal secretary is basically the same; it changes only as regards the relevant technology, from pencils to word processors, from hot sealing wax to stick-on labels.

Once she (or, occasionally, he) is hooked on legal work, there is no escape for the secretary. There is some prestige, there is much of interest and there are opportunities for advancement – major considerations when contemplating any career. Working in commerce or industry can sometimes be boring, although sometimes better paid but, from personal experience, documenting the life of a 'widget' from its factory birthplace to its showroom launch-pad is a potentially mind-numbing occupation. There is little human element and less interest. Of course, there are negative factors to legal work.

There can be acres of form filling, and clients who are boorish and condescending but, if you are interested in the human condition, you will find plenty in the legal world that is stimulating and challenging; not at all the dusty existence which outsiders may imagine. In today's competitive high-tech legal world, the accuracy and speed of service that clients require leave little time for cobwebs to appear.'

General office staff

Most firms of solicitors have a general office with staff consisting of messengers and clerks, whose job it is to collect and deliver papers, distribute incoming post, and collect up and frank outgoing mail. Sometimes the 'general office' is in charge of the firm's photocopying, and sometimes these staff act as receptionists as well. As a school-leaver, you could start in a general office without any very clear idea of what you want to do, or what alternatives are available to you, but having found your feet you might wish to move into other areas.

Outdoor clerks

In England and Wales and Northern Ireland, when solicitors tell clients they have issued a writ or taken out a summons, what they usually mean is that they have filled out the correct forms and handed them to the outdoor clerk who goes to the court and ensures that any necessary fees are paid and that the documents are stamped by the court. The outdoor clerk also lodges papers in court before hearings and obtains dates for court appointments. Sometimes applications for a hearing are simply put on a list and allocated a date by the court later, and in those cases it is up to the outdoor clerk to keep a check on the court lists and notify the solicitor when a hearing date is given. As an outdoor clerk becomes more experienced, he or she may also be asked to attend court on simple procedural applications. As an outdoor clerk, you would be out of the office most days of the week and would quickly learn both office and court procedure.

Outdoor clerks are often given their own files to work on. Very often they start off with debt collection matters, in which their knowledge of court procedure, and particularly of how judgments are enforced, is very useful. Some end up as managing clerks or go on to qualify as legal executives or solicitors, but others prefer to remain as outdoor clerks throughout their careers

There are no particular academic qualifications required, although you will need to be physically fit, have a good standard of spoken English, and be able to communicate well. Small firms may not employ an outdoor clerk and instead may ask a messenger to do the necessary work. However, most large firms that take on litigation work will produce enough court work to need an outdoor clerk. Salaries start from about £6,000. In Scotland most large firms employ messengers, but seldom employ outdoor clerks as those in England, Wales and Northern Ireland do.

Clerical staff

All firms have staff dealing with their accounting, and the size of the department will depend on the size of the firm. Some firms employ only one qualified accountant, while others have enough work to warrant taking on half-a-dozen school-leavers, as well as a number of qualified staff. Many firms now have computerized accounting systems, and you would have to be prepared to learn how to operate them, if necessary. Ilex Tutorial Services has introduced a legal accountancy course and exams in legal accountancy are held by the Institute of Legal Executives twice a year. Full details are available from the Institute (see Useful addresses).

Case Study

Brenda works as a credit controller in a solicitors' office.

'I have worked as a credit controller for 15 years. The first job I had was for a printing company. From there, I moved to a glass and glazing company, then on to a solicitors' office. This shows that as a credit controller, the main aim is to collect monies owed to the company – regardless of the product or service offered.

I would say the only difference working for a solicitors' office is that the accounting system differs slightly from that in the commercial sector, in that solicitors have a 'disbursement' account system from which they pay out funds on behalf of their clients and this amount is then included on the fee note eventually rendered.

As a credit controller, you always feel the need to get the bill paid. However, in the case of a house sale for instance, one may be told to hold the chasing pending the sale. Also, a fee earner dealing with probate matters for the firm often has to wait for money while the will goes through probate to allow access to the cleared funds and then to pay the bill.

To be a credit controller, you need to be computer literate, have a good working knowledge of accounts and a good telephone manner and to be able to work with and talk to people at the highest level in any company. Communication with clients is an everyday part of the job and there is a fine balance when talking to people; to always project the correct manner and deal with any difficulties they may have. While listening to their financial problems, at the same time you must also let them know the work has been done and we do expect to be paid. So the object is to collect payments, keep the clients happy and also the solicitor who originally raised the bill.'

Case Study

Julie works as a credit control assistant in a solicitors' office.

'I have worked for a solicitors' firm since the age of 17, starting as an office junior. My duties included photocopying, filing, relief switchboard, reception duties, deliveries, opening and franking daily mail, shredding documents and making myself generally useful around the office.

After two years I was moved to the firm's head office where my duties altered and I was given the position of junior typist/assistant receptionist taking the overflow of telephone calls from reception at my desk. I progressed from being an assistant receptionist to the Head Office receptionist within a few months and kept this position for nearly ten years. Starting out as an office junior, I feel, gave me a very good grounding for the subsequent position as Head Office receptionist, as it enabled me to gain an insight into the workings of the office from the ground up.

Working on reception, I acquired the crucial ability to deal and communicate with people at all levels – both clients and solicitors. I learned the importance of being diplomatic, for instance, when reassuring clients that solicitors would return calls and when solicitors made it clear that they did not want their work constantly to be interrupted by the telephone!

After ten years as a receptionist, I felt the need to widen my horizons and I subsequently applied to be moved to an administrative post. The practice manager offered me a position as his assistant/credit control assistant, which I found very challenging and enjoyable. My duties range from updating the internal and personnel records, inputting data on the computer and generally handling various enquiries. I am on hand for messages, telephone calls and any queries the practice manager may pass my way.'

4 The employers

Government Legal Service

The Government Legal Service (GLS) consists of the legal teams of about 25 separate central government departments and public bodies, who between them employ about 1100 solicitors and barristers. While some GLS lawyers can be employed in work similar to that found in private practice, including litigation and conveyancing, many GLS lawyers are involved in work which is unique to government, such as parliamentary drafting and advisory work and dealing with administrative and constitutional problems. Much of the work of the GLS is of a high profile nature. The GLS seeks 'students with a good mind and excellent communication skills, and the commitment to become a first class government lawyer'. Details on recruitment and further information about the GLS can be obtained from the GLS Recruitment Team (see useful addresses).

The Foreign and Commonwealth Office, the Parliamentary Counsel and the Northern Ireland Office legal teams do not form part of the GLS, but contact addresses are available from the GLS Recruitment Team. The Scottish Office legal team, which is managed separately, is based in Edinburgh, while information relating to Civil Service jobs in Northern Ireland can also be obtained from the Civil Service Commission in Londonderry.

The Prosecution Services

In all three jurisdictions, criminal prosecutions are now conducted on behalf of the State through lawyers employed by the government.

The Prosecution of Offences Act 1985 established in England and Wales for the first time the Crown Prosecution Service, which from 1 April 1986 took over responsibility for prosecutions (except for the very minor motoring offences known as 'specified proceedings') which had previously been undertaken by the police. Since the creation of the Crown Prosecution Service the job of the police has been restricted to that of investigating crime. It is the job of the legally qualified prosecutors to decide which cases should come to court and, where appropriate, to present the prosecution's case in court. The head of the service in England and Wales is the Director of Public Prosecutions and some 2000 prosecutors are employed in branch offices countrywide. One aim of the system is to ensure greater consistency in prosecuting practice throughout the country.

In Scotland the Crown Office is the Departmental Headquarters of the Procurator Fiscal Service, the body responsible for prosecutions in Scotland. The Scottish Law Officers – the Lord Advocate and the Solicitor General – are based in the Crown Office, which is also home base to Crown Counsel. The Head of Department is the Crown Agent.

The Procurator Fiscal is an independent public prosecutor who receives and considers reports of crimes and offences from the police and over 40 other agencies and decides whether or not to take criminal proceedings in the public interest. There are 49 Procurators Fiscal who with their Assistants and Deputies present cases in the Sheriffs' and District Courts throughout Scotland in a similar way to the Crown Prosecution Service. The more serious offences are prosecuted in the High Court by Crown Counsel who are members of the Faculty of Advocates.

In Northern Ireland, prosecutions are undertaken by the Director of Public Prosecutions for Northern Ireland, whose staff are legally qualified.

Local government

Local authorities throughout the UK employ many lawyers for a wide range of work. Some of their work, like that of civil servants, is akin to that carried on in private practice, such as conveyancing, planning and litigation, but even here the nature of the cases will be specialized – rather than buying and selling private homes, they may be in charge of letting or selling council houses; the planning might involve local road construction or industrial development. Equally, some work is peculiar to local government – lawyers will often be involved in public inquiries; assisting the social services with, for example, child care proceedings; and they also undertake personnel work for the council. Often, lawyers doing this sort of work will have decided on a job in local government early in their careers and will have specialized in their training accordingly, often having served a training contract with a local government department. This is not essential, and you might choose to work for a local authority having completed your training and obtained experience in private practice.

Jobs in local government are advertised in the national press and professional journals, and you could try applying direct to the local authorities in the areas in which you would like to work.

Magistrates' courts service

Magistrates' courts in England and Wales deal with 98 per cent of all criminal cases and have jurisdiction in respect of domestic, juvenile and licensing business. There are approximately 29,000 lay unpaid magistrates (justices of the peace) and about 60 stipendiary magistrates (who are legally qualified and salaried). While the lay magistrates are given training for their work, they require the assistance of a legally qualified court clerk to assist them in their understanding of the law when reaching their decisions.

Justices' clerks advise the lay magistrates on law, practice and procedure and are also responsible for the administration of the local magistrates' courts service. There are over 200 justices' clerks and about 10,500 members of staff in the magistrates' courts service. A justices' clerk must be a solicitor or barrister of at least five years' standing with experience in a justices' clerk's office.

Apart from the justices' clerk, the magistrates' courts service employs a considerable number of solicitors and barristers, many of whom receive their training as such while serving as trainees in the service, although others obtain these qualifications beforehand. Appropriate leave and financial assistance are usually provided to enable trainees to qualify as solicitors or barristers.

In Scotland, District Courts are administered by local authorities. Clerks in the Scottish Court Service are non-legal staff at the court of session, the High Court of Justiciary and the sheriff court.

In Northern Ireland there are no lay magistrates, and there is therefore no equivalent to the office of justices' clerk.

Industry and commerce

Industrial and commercial institutions, public bodies, and business organizations of all kinds employ lawyers. Many solicitors and barristers are attracted by the prospect of a career in business. If you go to work in industry, the areas of law you will deal with will depend on the nature of the organization that you join. If your employer is a retailer, whether marketing pharmaceuticals, cars or high fashion, you will undoubtedly need to advise on consumer legislation; if your employer exports anything from books to bottled beer you will have to explain the requirements of international and EU law, and help resolve disputes over shipping agreements and the carriage of the goods. In all cases you are likely to become involved with problems at a much earlier stage than you would in private practice, which can make the job more interesting and constructive. The Law Society's Careers and Recruitment Service and the Bar Association for Commerce, Finance and Industry (BACFI) publish useful information about the work that in-house lawyers do.

Although it is difficult to generalize about the type of job you could find yourself doing, to succeed in the business world you are going to need commercial sense and an ability to find practical solutions as well as legal answers. As your employer will also be your client, you will need to be able to react quickly to situations as they arise, and as your input will only be part of the equation you will probably be called upon to work alongside other professionals, such as accountants, personnel officers, financial advisers and marketing directors, to resolve problems.

If you are thinking of a career in industry you should consider very carefully where your interests lie, and then try to find out as much as possible about the workings of the organizations to which you intend to apply. Vacancies in industry are advertised in the *Law Society's Gazette*, the *Journal of the Law Society of Scotland*, and on a notice board in the Inns of Court. In addition, companies advertise in the national and legal press, and BACFI circulates details to members. Some employers also recruit through employment agencies.

Work in industry could take you anywhere in the UK, for although in the past large companies have tended to be based in cities, there has been considerable decentralization in recent years and head offices are now to be found throughout the provinces.

Remuneration in industry tends to involve a package of salary and benefits, such as a company car, a pension scheme, bonuses and possibly subsidized mortgages and loans. As a result, the overall remuneration is sometimes higher in this type of job than in a similar position in private practice.

Case Study

***Bill** is the Director of Legal Services and Company Secretary of a major company in a shipping-related industry.*

'The company employs two solicitors, an assistant secretary and two legal assistants. The department as a whole is involved in a wide range of matters including company or commercial, property, environmental, parliamentary, litigation, employment, debt collection and personal injury. I deal mainly with company or commercial, property, environmental and parliamentary matters. I am also responsible for the company share registration and claims sections.

I was attracted to the position of an in-house lawyer because I was looking for a more direct and closer participation in industry or commerce. I also had a particular interest in my chosen industry. Prior to joining my present company, I had taken a law degree at Bristol followed by the then Solicitors Finals before joining a general private practice firm. Some two years after I had qualified with that firm, I moved to my present company. I am now its Director of Legal Services and Company Secretary.

The key benefits that I perceive for an in-house lawyer are, first, job satisfaction obtained, for example, by being closely involved with a project, seeing it through from its inception to completion and then, where appropriate, continuing to be involved with it during its existence. Second, there is the wide range of work and situations that I come across. This in turn creates a challenging environment in which to work. The growing impact of new legislation on companies gives the in-house lawyer a much more pro-active role in advising the business on the strategy to deal with the legislation. Where matters are placed outside, I assume responsibility for monitoring and liaising with the external solicitors.

Although I have mentioned variety of work as an advantage, it is equally possible for somebody who so wishes to specialize in a very particular field. There are in-house solicitors in, for example, telecommunications, banking, energy and licensing who acquire a highly specialized knowledge and can be experts in their field. In my experience, a company that seeks to employ an in-house solicitor is looking for someone with a common-sense approach to legal matters and who will have or will acquire a greater understanding and appreciation of business. Given the importance of corporate governance, those who become in-house solicitors who are involved in this field should be able to express strong and independent viewpoints where necessary. It is important to remember that in private practice a dissatisfied client usually moves to another firm. In industry, it is you who moves if the client becomes dissatisfied.

I find the work more stimulating and absorbing than I did in private practice. One of the attractions for an in-house solicitor is of course the ability, should he or she wish, to move into other areas of management. The legal department can be a stepping stone to higher management and ultimately the board of a company where a lawyer's analytical mind, independence and ability to look at both sides of an argument are valuable attributes.'

Law Centres

The first Law Centre was set up in 1970 in North Kensington in London and now there are more than 50 throughout the country, particularly in deprived inner-city areas. They grew up initially in response to local needs for free legal advice and representation for individuals and groups, and they still serve these needs. Law Centres are not sufficiently resourced to work with all the people that come to them; they concentrate on those areas in which they see the greatest local need. Some of the most common areas of work are: housing, eg tenants' rights and homelessness, welfare rights, employment, eg industrial tribunals, planning and environment, children's rights, juvenile crime, education and anti-discrimination work. Some Law Centres also provide a 24-hour emergency service covering detentions by the police, deportations, domestic violence and action against unlawful evictions.

Law Centres consciously make the legal processes and systems less obscure to people. They employ not only legally qualified people but also expert advice workers and community workers to ensure a more welcoming and less intimidating style of work. Law Centres are responsive to the needs of the people within their communities; they help, advise and represent people in a number of ways. This includes development work, such as enabling community-based groups to start up in response to a legal issue in the local area and carrying out casework for groups of individuals with the same problem. They offer training and education, eg taking in students and volunteers from the local area. Law Centres also carry out research and respond to proposals put forward by government, local authorities or other bodies that affect people in the local area, or that are issues of public interest.

Law Centres are accountable to their local communities and are run by a locally elected management committee, made up of interested individuals and organizations from the area. Management committees are voluntary and members give their time free; they may also have representatives from the local Law Society. All Law Centres are non-profit-making. Most are funded by their local authority although a few have grant aid from the Legal Aid Board. Many are increasingly having to rely on legal aid income and support from charities.

Jobs in Law Centres are advertised in the national press and in the Legal Action Group Bulletin as well as in specialist journals. Information about work in a Law Centre can be obtained from the Law Centres Federation.

Citizens' Advice Bureaux

Citizens' Advice Bureaux (CABs) were opened in 1939 to assist members of the public who were in need of help. Most large towns now have a CAB, funded partly by local government and partly by central government and Charities. There are at present more than 1000 CABs in England and Wales, and just under 100 in Scotland and Northern Ireland.

A very small number of CABs in England and Wales employ their own lawyers, both to act as specialist advisers to the rest of the team and also to undertake their own cases on behalf of the bureau's clients. CAB community lawyers are usually solicitors, although barristers have also been employed. The type of case they will see depends on the locality in which the bureau is situated. If the bureau is in a middle-class suburb it is likely that the community lawyer will tend to deal with neighbour disputes and consumer problems, whereas if the bureau is in a deprived inner-city area it is likely that the community lawyer will be involved with such problems as social welfare law, employment, housing and immigration. The policy of CABs is to respond to the needs of the community as they arise.

Unfortunately, CABs and many other advice agencies are at present facing difficulties over funding, but if you are interested in considering this area of work you should contact your local CAB, or the Greater London CAB Service (for London) or the National Association of CAB (for England and Wales), or Citizens' Advice Scotland or the Northern Ireland Association of CAB.

All CABs in Northern Ireland, and many others throughout the UK, rely on lawyers giving help on a voluntary basis and you might find it interesting to attend voluntary sessions to find out whether the work would appeal to you, or simply to be of help to the community.

The Lord Chancellor's Department

The Lord Chancellor's Department is a major government department with wide responsibilities for the administration of justice in England and Wales. Since 1972 it has been responsible for the day-to-day administration of all the higher courts, ie County and Crown Courts, the High Court and Court of Appeal. It also has policy responsibilities for magistrates' courts, although administration on a day-to-day basis is carried out locally.

The running of the 400 or more courts that fall within the Department's responsibility could clearly not all be handled from London, where the Department has its headquarters, and so for this purpose the country (ie England and Wales – the Scottish Court Service is administered by the Scottish Courts Administration and the courts in Northern Ireland by the Northern Ireland Court Service) is divided into six regional areas which are known as 'Circuits'. Each Circuit is headed by a senior official of the 'Circuit Administrator'- who is responsible for the smooth running of the groups of courts within his area. Approximately 8000 of the Department's staff work in the regions and are directly involved in the day-to-day business of the courts; the remainder work in London.

5 Allied professions

Teachers

Some lawyers prefer to teach rather than practise in the main-stream of the legal profession. The level of academic qualifications required varies depending on the level at which you wish to teach. University lecturers usually have a first class or upper second class LLB or BA, and the majority will also have a Masters degree and a professional qualification. However, law is also taught in colleges of further education, both separately and as part of other courses, and in these cases the academic require-ments for teachers may not be so high.

Professional colleges, such as the College of Law and the Inns of Court School of Law in England and Wales and the Institute of Professional Legal Studies in Northern Ireland, also employ teachers. In these there will be greater emphasis on the teachers' understanding of the requirements of the profession which the student is to enter.

The universities advertise their vacancies in the national press, and details of vacancies can be obtained directly from the colleges or departments. In the case of colleges of further education, information can be obtained from the Local Education Authority in the area in which the college is situated. Some colleges adver-tise posts in professional magazines, such as the *Law Society's Gazette* and the *Journal of the Law Society of Scotland*.

If you want to teach law, you will need more than a good degree. You must have a genuine interest in the subject area you are going to teach, as well as a wish to communicate your enthusiasm to others. Certainly, at higher levels of education you will need an interest in ideas for their own sake, as well as an ability to lecture and write. Many people think of teaching as an easy option which gives secure employment and long holidays. However, teaching has its own problems (such as keeping up to date with the subject material) and you should make sure before you set out that you know the genuine advantages and disadvantages of the job.

The pressures of teaching are usually less than those experienced by barristers and advocates and solicitors but they do exist. Many teachers have to be prepared to teach for five hours a day and, like any stand-up comic, they can die on their audience! Also, the jobs, while relatively secure and pensioned, usually pay only two-thirds as much as is earned by solicitors or barristers and advocates with comparable experience. Like all jobs, teaching has its boring moments, and most teachers dread the annual round of setting examinations and marking papers.

Teachers probably have greater control than barristers and advocates or solicitors over the way they spend their days, and they also have the advantage that their skills can more readily be transferred to other countries outside the UK.

Company secretaries and chartered secretaries

The role of a company secretary is one recognized in legislation, which requires that company secretaries of public limited companies be professionally qualified. This places the company secretary in a unique position *vis-à-vis* the board of directors. The company secretary is the officer who is ostensibly the company's chief administrator. However, a company secretary's actual function will vary from company to company.

Company secretaries, whether of public or private companies, deal with aspects of management which relate to the company as a legal entity. They keep the company records, make the company's tax returns, advise the board of directors of their legal obligations and arrange company meetings, collect information for the meetings and record their decisions. In many companies, the company secretary will have a direct legal or financial function and will possibly also be involved in personnel management. Company secretaries are administrators who assist in management, planning and the general running of the company.

As the responsibilities and needs of the job have grown, the role has been established on a more professional basis. Many company secretaries in private companies have legal qualifications and many others, particularly in larger organizations, are members of the Institute of Chartered Secretaries and Administrators, which holds exams in June and December of each year leading to the qualification of Chartered Secretary. Opportunities for chartered secretaries are considerable, as the skills they have are required by many organizations and there is plenty of scope for specialization and moving into general management and administration at the highest level. Full details of the training and qualifications of chartered secretaries are available from the Institute (see Useful addresses).

Patent agents

There are currently some 1250 patent agents on the UK Register of Patent Agents and, while there is no requirement for them to have formal legal qualifications, their work involves a considerable knowledge of the law of patents, copyright and trademarks, both here and abroad.

The government runs the Patent Office as part of the Department of Trade and Industry. This deals with about 40,000 applications per year from inventors who want a patent granted for their invention. The grant of patent means that an inventor can stop people using his or her invention without permission for 20 years. The growing complexity of the system of registration, added to the fact that inventors are now more commonly companies than private individuals, has led to the growth of a small profession of people whose primary function is to act on behalf of inventors in registering their inventions both with the UK Patent Office and abroad.

The work of a patent agent involves drafting and revising patent specifications and licence agreements. A patent agent will often be asked to advise on the validity of patents or on whether a patent or trademark is being infringed. It is not at all uncommon for patent agents to bring proceedings on behalf of clients where there has been an infringement, and some will even appear for clients in the Patent Court, on appeals from decisions of the Patent Office, rather than engage barristers to do so.

To be a patent agent requires a rather unusual blend of skills: legal, linguistic and technical. Most patent agents have a degree in a science subject and receive in-house training at work. For those who make the grade it can be both interesting and financially rewarding. Further details can be obtained from the Chartered Institute of Patent Agents (see Useful addresses).

Notaries

Notaries are public officers who are appointed to draw up, authenticate and certify deeds and documents, such as conveyances and powers of attorney which concern property, or are to take effect, abroad. They are also called upon to certify transactions relating to negotiable instruments (for example, bills of exchange) when there is a foreign element to the transaction. They are appointed by the Court of Faculties of the Archbishop of Canterbury, but with the exception of ecclesiastical notaries, they are not concerned with church matters.

A notary's certificate on any document is important, since it is recognized anywhere in the world. Notaries are often called upon to witness signatures on legal documents, and they are also able to prepare wills and other important legal papers.

There are three types of notary, ecclesiastical notaries who are usually diocesan registrars or legal secretaries to bishops, scrivener notaries and general notaries. Scrivener notaries constitute a very small, separate profession practising in central London. No other notaries are authorized to practise in that area. They have their own training system, which involves serving an apprenticeship of five years with a practising notary, and taking exams in

English legal subjects, foreign languages and foreign law. One year of their apprenticeship is served abroad. The standard required for those wishing to train as scrivener notaries is high, and the openings are few. Enquiries should be addressed to the Society of Public Notaries of London (see Useful addresses).

General notaries, who are normally also solicitors, can practise in all parts of England and Wales outside central London. Prior to admission they have to sit various examinations set by the Court of Faculties.

In Scotland if you wish to be a public notary you must first be enrolled as a solicitor and then petition the Inner House of the Court of Session. Most practising newly qualified Scottish solicitors become notaries.

Recruitment consultants

More and more employers within the legal profession are recognizing the importance of recruiting the right people to work for them. Making a mistake can prove difficult and costly to solve. As a result, opportunities for recruitment specialists to service the needs of such employers, as well as the needs of job seekers, have increased steadily in recent years.

Case Study

Tuesday *is 31 and a director of a legal recruitment consultancy.*

'My route into legal recruitment consultancy was not premeditated. Having started a career in press and public relations for the IT industry, I moved into commercial sales recruitment following relocation to the North West of England. The recruitment business in the sales sector is highly competitive with success coming as much from sheer graft as from a knowledge of the market, which is extremely diverse, and I wanted something different.

I began to look for an area in which to specialize, where an in-depth understanding of the recruiters and those seeking placements might reap real rewards. A combination of my law studies at college and research into the North West jobs market led me to join the legal division of a national recruitment group.

Getting started in the business was not easy. I had to develop a wide knowledge of the requirements and, importantly, the culture of firms of all sizes at the same time as building a candidate-base to match these requirements. Having some personal contacts within the legal profession was certainly an advantage, but in a market dominated by a few agencies and individuals it took a lot of effort to make a name for myself while meeting tough financial targets. Within a short time I had been successful enough to be looking for greater rewards from my employer and join another national agency on a better package. As with any role with a sales element, you buy yourself increasing responsibility and rewards on the basis of the reputation you build.

By this time, a significant proportion of the candidates I was placing came to me through personal recommendation. This is critical for a recruitment consultant, as there are many agencies in the market and advertising for candidates is both hit and miss and expensive. Within a fairly closed business community like the law, word of mouth is the most effective form of marketing. Not only did I find that solicitors would recommend me to friends looking to move, but that many that I had placed in the past had achieved partner level and hence came to me as recruiters.

I moved into a management role within the same company, running a small but profitable office of legal recruitment consultants. For me, management responsibility was a double-edged sword, as I needed to focus on developing others and fulfilling the reporting and planning aspects of my role as well as on fee earning from satisfied clients and candidates. The experience was useful – things were going well but I now knew I wanted to run my own business.

I went into partnership with another successful consultant working in a local agency but starting up the company was very stressful. In the current economic climate prospective backers are, to say the least, extremely cautious. With perseverance and much planning we got it off the ground and now run a very successful consultancy.

I think the key to being an effective and successful legal recruitment consultant is to know your market inside out, to understand what the firms need and what the candidates want, and then have the ability to match like with like. Above all, self-motivation and the ability to persuade and negotiate are key to this role.'

6

Qualifications and Getting Started

Training for solicitors

The training requirements for solicitors vary between the three jurisdictions of England and Wales, Scotland and Northern Ireland. Solicitors qualifying in one jurisdiction do not automatically qualify to practise in either of the other two, but each jurisdiction provides a test for those already qualified elsewhere in the UK. For example, the Law Society of Scotland provides an Intra UK Transfer Test for fully qualified solicitors from England, Wales and Northern Ireland who wish to qualify in Scotland also. Northern Ireland, England and Wales now have a reciprocal agreement whereby they recognize each other's qualified solicitors. Thus, once you are qualified as a solicitor in Northern Ireland you can apply for admission as a solicitor in England and Wales without need for further examination or qualification and vice versa.

In all three jurisdictions, the profession is open to graduates and non-graduates alike, but it should be noted that well over 90 per cent of solicitors throughout the UK graduate before commencing their professional training. To qualify as a non-graduate is more time-consuming and more difficult, in that it necessitates studying while in employment, and many employers prefer to take on trainees who have a degree.

Training in England and Wales

Training requirements are laid down by the Law Society from whom full details may be obtained, but if you decide to become a solicitor the first thing to think about is what route you wish to follow to qualify, as there are several to choose from. Although those entering the profession are mostly graduates, and in general, the prospects for graduates tend to be better, you do not need to have a law degree, or any degree at all. You may choose to start training immediately on leaving school with A–levels. The three main categories of trainee are: law graduates; non-law graduates; and (to a much lesser extent) Fellows of the Institute of Legal Executives (see pages 71–2).

Academic training

The main route to becoming a solicitor is the law degree route. If you decide to take a law degree, you will need to achieve three good passes at A–level, because competition for places on law degree courses is intense. You may study any academic subjects, the crucial requirement being to obtain good grades, ie grade C or better. You should ensure that within your law degree you cover the seven Foundations of Legal Knowledge required by both the Law Society and the Inns of Court to complete the academic side of training. Applications for places on law degree courses are made via the University Admission Services.

If you obtain a degree in a subject other than law you will have to follow a course leading to the CPE which covers the core subjects taken as part of most law degrees, such as constitutional law, contract, tort, criminal law, land law and equity and trusts, or alternatively the course which leads to the postgraduate Diploma in Law. For Law Society purposes, there is no difference. Non-law graduates usually have to pass six papers and mature students eight papers. There are recognized courses leading to the CPE exams and details are obtainable from the Law Society. Partial exemptions are available for Fellows of the Institute of Legal Executives.

Vocational training

The Law Society's Final Examination Course for solicitors has now been replaced by a more practical Legal Practice Course (LPC). The course is taught and assessed by approved institutions subject to the Law Society's supervision exercised through the Legal Practice Course Board. The Board is responsible for monitoring the quality of the course.

The purpose of the course is to ensure that trainee solicitors entering training contracts have the necessary knowledge and skills to undertake appropriate tasks under proper supervision during the contract. A full-time LPC runs for one academic year, a part-time course for two years. The introduction of part-time courses has increased the flexibility of the training scheme and access to the profession. The Competition for places on the LPC is stiff and candidates need good academic qualifications.

The Training Regulations now permit institutions to offer an integrated course which combines the academic stage core subjects and the Legal Practice Course in a two-year programme of study. Also, teaching institutions may apply to run four-year exempting law degrees which combine a qualifying law degree with a Legal Practice Course. Before a student can commence the LPC, he or she must apply for student membership of the Law Society.

Allocation of places

Application forms for full-time courses are available from September until the beginning of December in the year prior to your wanting a place and can be obtained from the LPC Applications Board, PO Box 84, Guildford, Surrey GU3 1YX. It is your responsibility to ensure that your application is submitted before the closing date. Students wishing to apply for a part-time course must apply directly to the institutions that offer this.

Financial support

The Law Society provides helpful information, notably in its guide *The Law Degree Route to Qualification as a Solicitor*, on financial support for students taking the CPE or LPC.

Student membership of the Law Society

In accordance with the Law Society's Training Regulations 1990, no person may commence a Legal Practice Course or enter into a Training Contract unless he or she has been issued with a Certificate of Student Enrolment. In addition, no student may commence a Legal Practice Course until he or she has obtained from the Law Society a Certificate of Completion of the Academic Stage of Training.

A composite application form for Student Enrolment and for a Certificate of Completion of the Academic Stage of Training may be obtained from the Regulation Enquiries branch of the Law Society at its Redditch office (see Useful addresses).

Finding a training contract

You will also need to start applying for a training contract and attend interviews. Many private practice employers will recruit trainee solicitors up to two years in advance. You should therefore contact your prospective employer as early as possible, to find out what their requirements are. You will need to bear in mind the fact that the profession is very competitive and entry into it is by no means guaranteed to those with law degrees, CPE or LAC. Economic circumstances alone mean that training places within the profession are subject to market forces that can fluctuate. Many fully qualified solicitors are also facing or have faced redundancy, so the situation is not confined to trainees.

You must also be aware of the need to market yourself. It is a competitive world, so you must create opportunities to get a job and use every opportunity carefully to your advantage. You must have good interpersonal skills. A solicitor must be able to communicate with clients at every level, by letter, in person and on the telephone.

The training contract

After a successful completion of the academic and vocational stages, you will have to undergo a period of practical training, which is a two-year training contract in England and Wales, with an authorized firm of solicitors or other such organization. This is to enable the trainee solicitor to gain experience of the practical aspects of a solicitor's work. During the training contract, the candidate has to undertake a 20-day Professional Skills Course, which is modular in nature and can be undertaken at various points of the training contract, through various means of training. This period of training used to be called Articles, but is now referred to as a training contract.

When it comes to finding a training contract, the onus is on you, the candidate. Many firms recruit two years in advance and vacancies are notified to universities where potential trainees can be found. In addition, most firms will register a vacancy in the appropriate directories and the Law Society produces a directory called ROSET (Register of Solicitors Employing Trainees) which is available from the Law Society and from many universities. This enables the candidate to see which firms are offering vacancies and to contact them directly. Some firms visit universities to interview final year students, but this practice is at present decreasing and many employers prefer to interview candidates on their own premises.

Competition for training contracts is great, and prospective trainees should be aware of the need to apply at an early stage. They need good academic qualifications and languages or computer skills may help to give them the edge in any applications. It is essential to research thoroughly the firms to which you are applying, and to ensure that each application is tailored to that particular organization.

As part of the training contract the Law Society requires firms to give trainees experience of at least three areas of law. Obviously, not all firms offer the same areas of law, so you have to decide when applying to a firm the kind of law you wish to practise and the kind of client you wish to deal with. Failure to gain experience in your preferred areas of law during your training contract may make it more difficult for you to obtain work in that area subsequently.

The Law Society requires firms to pay trainees a minimum salary and this requirement has continued for some time, although some solicitors argue that it reduces the number of training contracts available. However, many firms pay well above the minimum and pay salaries which compare favourably with those of other fields of graduate employment. A 'fundamental review' by the Law Society of training contracts was launched in 1997: the question of the minimum salary is one of the matters to be put on the agenda, but at the very least the minimum salary will be retained until 1999.

Training in Scotland

Solicitors in Scotland have their names inserted on a Roll of Solicitors and are granted annual Certificates entitling them to practise by the Law Society of Scotland. A Certificate is granted to candidates who are at least 21, have completed a term of practical training and have passed approved exams. The Law Society of Scotland will be happy to provide its *Careers Information* booklet on request.

The academic training of law in Scotland is largely undertaken by five of the universities. Thus 97 per cent of those who qualify as solicitors in Scotland do so by taking an LLB (Ordinary or Honours), or an Arts degree followed by an LLB, at a Scottish university, followed by the Diploma in Legal Practice, and a period of in-office training.

Non-law graduates may take the Professional Exams of the Law Society; appropriate university classes may be taken, but this is not obligatory and depends on the availability of places at the university. Entrants to the Professional Exams must have the appropriate GCE A level or SCE H Grade (or equivalent) passes. The Professional Exams are as follows: Public Law and the Legal System; Scots Private Law; Scots Commercial Law; Evidence; Conveyancing; Taxation; Scots Criminal Law; European Community Law. The exams may be taken separately or together in any order but, where a candidate is undergoing pre-Diploma training, the exams must be passed within a period of four years. The LLB from a Scottish university gives total exemption from the exams provided it contains all the necessary subjects.

It is now necessary for all intending entrants, graduates and non-graduates to the profession in Scotland to obtain the Diploma in Legal Practice, after the completion of the LLB degree or the Law Society's Professional Exams. The Diploma is a university award, obtained after one year of full-time study and provides training in the practical skills required by solicitors. The Diploma course is followed by a two-year training contract in a solicitor's office, during the latter year of which the trainee is entitled to hold a restricted practising certificate, enabling him or her to appear in court. Trainee solicitors are normally paid at a mutually agreed rate based on scales recommended by the Law Society of Scotland.

A solicitor admitted in Scotland may immediately apply to sit the Legal Practice Course to qualify for practice in England and Wales.

Training in Northern Ireland

The solicitors' professional body in Northern Ireland is the Law Society of Northern Ireland. It has overall responsibility for education and admission to the profession and it provides *Notes For Guidance Of Intending Students* which provide helpful information.

Admission to training is generally dependent on possession of a degree from a recognized university. Law graduates must attend a two-year vocational apprenticeship course, of which the academic year is spent at the Institute of Professional Legal Studies at the Queen's University of Belfast, after which they may be admitted as solicitors, but they are not licensed to practise on their own account until they have served for three years as the qualified assistant of a practising solicitor. Other graduates must complete a two-year full-time academic course in law at the Law Faculty, followed by the two-year vocational apprenticeship course, and may then be admitted on the same conditions as indicated above.

On qualifying

In England and Wales, once your training is completed and provided you are at least 21 years old, your name will be entered on the Roll of Solicitors and you will be eligible to apply for an annual Practising Certificate. You may also become a member of the Law Society, although membership is not compulsory.

In Scotland the Council of the Society petitions the Court of Session for admission of trainees and once the petition is granted, your name will be entered on the Roll of Solicitors kept by the Law Society of Scotland, and again you will then be entitled to apply for a Practising Certificate. This is permissible after one year of training, whereupon a restricted practising certificate is granted, allowing the second-year trainee to appear in the law courts.

In Northern Ireland, you apply for admission, and your name is entered on the Roll maintained by the Law Society of Northern Ireland.

Case Study

Rod *is a 29-year-old trainee who turned to the law after originally working as a graduate in local government. He works for a 14-partner firm with five offices in the North West and a broad general practice.*

My training over the two-year period is divided between four departments: civil litigation, conveyancing, commercial and matrimonial law.

Initially, if one has not previously worked in an office environment, a trainee must familiarize him or herself with office procedures, and must also master the art of dealing with clients face to face.

My first six months were spent within the civil litigation department at one of the firm's branch offices. I soon became experienced in taking instructions from and advising clients, both legally aided and privately paying, in the fields of personal injury, consumer and contractual disputes. I attended many interlocutory hearings and often sat behind counsel during county court trials.

By the end of that time I felt reasonably confident with the work, but I then began a very different regime in the conveyancing department. This was equally busy, but perhaps more predictable, and I gained experience in dealing with house sales and purchases from start to finish.

Within the commercial department my training is based more on observing, sitting in on meetings, reading files and research, eg on points of company and employment law. There is understandably less client contact, as many business clients require their work to be handled at partner level. Even so, it is still possible to learn a great deal.

My only reservation about moving around departments is that, just as you become familiar with the work, it is time to move on. On the other hand, it is vital to obtain good quality experience over as wide a field as possible while training, and that might prove more difficult in a smaller firm, for example one with little commercial work. At least my experience should enable me to make career choices on a reasonably firm foundation.'

Salary

Many firms offer trainees work after they have completed their training contract, but others do not. It is prudent to start trying to secure a post-qualification job six months before the training contract is due to end.

Your salary on qualifying can vary depending on your academic record and experience. It also depends on whether the firm is offering partnership prospects and considers you have partnership potential, what sort of work you will be doing, and where you will be working. If you specialize in commercial work, shipping law, computer contracts or tax you should expect to be offered more than solicitors specializing in conveyancing or matrimonial work. But this is not a hard and fast rule, and specialists of any sort in a city will probably earn more than general practitioners, wherever they practise. Also, it is generally, but not exclusively, the case that larger city firms will pay more than small firms in the country. The legal profession is, of course, subject to general economic pressures, and at times of economic stringency certain specializations will fare less well and hence pay less well than others.

Money is not all a firm will be offering. The package includes holiday entitlement (usually four weeks), and may also include medical insurance schemes, pension schemes, interest-free loan facilities and bonuses. You should bear in mind what the firm has to offer in terms of office environment, equipment and secretarial assistance. Remember, you are going to be in your office for around 48 weeks of every year for at least eight hours a day. Therefore money cannot be your sole consideration when deciding to take on the job of a solicitor.

If you are a Law Graduate	If you are a Non-law Graduate	If you are a Non-Graduate
A–levels	A–levels	GCSE (or mature student over 25 years)
Degree in Law	Degree in any subject	Enter legal employment and register with Institute of Legal Executives ILEX Part 1 Examinations (approx. 2 years)
Legal Practice Course (1 year full-time or 2 years part-time)	Common Professional Examination or post-graduate diploma in law (1 year full-time or 2 years part-time)	ILEX Part II Examination (including 3 Foundation Subjects of CPE). Admitted to Membership of Institute of Legal Executives
2 years Training contract and Professional Skills Course	Legal Practice Course (1 year full-time or 2 years part-time)	
	2 years Training contract and Professional Skills Course	2 years further legal experience and 4 remaining foundation subjects plus one optional substantive law paper taken from ILEX Part II examination.

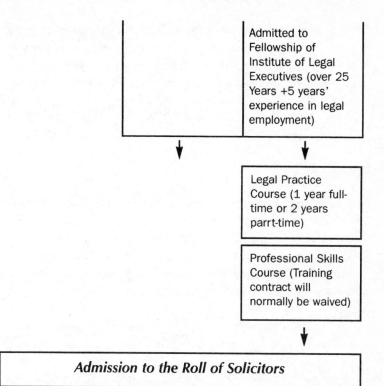

Qualifying as a solicitor in England and Wales
(*Source*: The Law Society)

Training for barristers

England and Wales

The academic stage usually consists of either a law degree or a degree in another subject supplemented by a one-year 'conversion course'. This could take the form of the Common Professional Examination (CPE) or a diploma in law. You will normally need to have a minimum of a 2.2, whether your degree is in law or not.

During the academic stage you will have to study foundations of legal knowledge. If your law degree does not cover all of these, for example, if you choose other options or if you study law with another subject, you will have to complete the relevant parts of the CPE or diploma before passing on to the next stage of training. If you are following a modular degree programme in, for example, combined studies, you should consult your tutor to ensure that the 'pathway' you follow will meet the Bar's requirements.

Joining an Inn

Before passing on to the next stage, it is recommended that you should become a member of an Inn of Court (although you may have done so at an earlier point in the academic stage). You can only apply to join one Inn. All offer roughly the same support: a library, educational activities, mooting societies, somewhere to eat, common rooms, gardens. More importantly they all have a senior member of staff to deal with students and pupils. The Inns all run 'sponsorship' schemes too. These link students with senior barristers in relevant areas of specialization – another valuable source of information.

Your choice of Inn may therefore be guided by issues such as atmosphere and character or, on a more practical note, the number and size of scholarships and awards on offer. Different Inns have different awards and scholarships to suit different needs.

Mini-pupillages

During the academic stage of training, you should try to get some further insight into the work of a barrister. You do this through mini-pupillages – two or three are probably sufficient. These usually take the form of a week's work experience and work shadowing: reading papers, discussing cases, attending court – even completing some written work. Mini-pupillages are an important part of deciding whether life as a barrister would suit you and, if so, which areas of specialization interest you. In some chambers, they may form part of the selection process for real pupillages. If you don't do a mini-pupillage, for whatever reason, you should at the very least aim to attend court a few times.

The vocational stage consists of a one-year course; the Bar Vocational Course (BVC). Traditionally, the BVC has been available at only one institution, the Inns of Court School of Law in London. However, since September 1997 it has also been offered by a few, carefully selected institutions in other parts of the country. Applications are made through a centralized clearing system known as CACH (Centralised Applications and Clearing House), and it is also possible to do the course on a part-time basis over two years.

You should aim to gain as much relevant experience and knowledge as you can during the vocational stage. This might include: debating, mooting (holding mock trials), work for a Citizens' Advice Bureau or the Free Representation Unit, attending court, marshalling (shadowing a judge) and further mini-pupillages.

Course content

Unlike the courses which make up the academic stage of training, the Bar Vocational Course places a 60 per cent emphasis on skills, with only 40 per cent of the year's work covering knowledge. The other major elements of the course are professional conduct and two specialist options.

In many classes students play an active part, which often involves role-playing exercises. They may find themselves interviewing one another, negotiating solutions to legal problems, even enacting court procedures, as well as drafting documents and written recommendations. Some exercises may be based on briefs similar to those that barristers deal with in the early years of practice. Both the skills and knowledge elements of the course emphasize the need for a professional approach to work. To lay the foundations for this, the course will include classes on professional conduct.

Pupillage

Pupillage generally takes one year, although it is split into six-month periods or 'sixes'. You can choose to do your first and second sixes at two different sets of chambers rather than one if you wish. Neither route guarantees that you will obtain a tenancy (a permanent place in chambers). In fact, 'third sixes', undertaken by those who fail to become tenants at the first attempt, are becoming increasingly commonplace. At present, there are a small number of pupillages at the employed Bar (that is, work as a legal adviser for an employer, rather than in independent practice).

Training and experience

All pupils are assigned to one or more pupilmasters or pupilmistresses, experienced barristers who organize training, allocate work and assess performance. Pupillages also give chambers the opportunity to assess pupils with a view to ensuring that they become effective practitioners.

Pupillage is hard work. The first six generally consists of observing and assisting your pupilmaster or pupilmistress and other barristers from chambers. There will be a great deal of research, together with document writing and document reading. At the end of a satisfactory first six, you receive a certificate enabling you to take on work of your own. The transition to the second six is therefore significant. This is where you start to build your own reputation. You have cases of your own, clients of your own, court appearances on your own – resulting in cases won or cases lost.

A certain amount of training takes place outside the environment of chambers. The Bar Council requires all pupils to attend two compulsory courses. The first gives further training in advocacy and the second practical help with managing a practice, including advice on financial issues. There are also voluntary, but highly recommended courses in accountancy and EU law.

Money matters

Nowadays, chambers fund over half of pupillages, occasionally to levels comparable with graduate starting salaries in other fields. The Inns of Court also provide a limited number of awards for members in their pupillage year, while the Bar Council offers a small number of interest-free loans. You may get the opportunity to supplement these sources of funding through work of your own during your second six. However, you may have accumulated large amounts of debt during the academic and vocational stages, and even if you get a tenancy, you will be looking forward to a future of self-employment which will not offer guaranteed levels of earnings.

You will therefore need to do some long-term financial planning well before you get to the pupillage stage. Don't count on getting substantial funding for pupillage – if anything at all.

Applying for pupillage

When applying for pupillage you should be guided first and foremost by the areas of practice which most interest you. You will find that some chambers cover a broad range of legal areas, while others are more narrowly specialized. Because you have to apply for pupillage so early (between the academic and vocational stages), it can be difficult to know exactly which areas of the law interests you. However, you will have the academic stage more or less behind you and you should have completed one or more mini-pupillages by the time you apply. There may also be pupillage fairs to help you find out more about several sets of chambers at once and to meet people you might be working with. The Bar Council publishes the *Chambers, Pupillages and Awards Handbook*, which gives potential applicants all the information they need, (see Useful addresses).

Applying for pupillage has been made easier and fairer by the introduction of PACH (the Pupillage Applications Clearing House) run by the Bar Council. This is a centralized system of applications, which forwards your details to up to 20 sets of chambers on completion of a simple disk-based application form. In addition, you can apply on an individual basis to the minority of chambers not participating in the scheme.

The other important feature of the PACH system is its synchronized timetable for applications, interviews, offers and acceptances. The advantage of the system is that potential pupils are not left to juggle offers of places, while waiting to hear from their first-choice chambers. Another benefit is that after the closing date for acceptances PACH operates a pool system to match applicants without places to chambers with unfilled pupillages.

Obtaining a tenancy

Although pupillage is the principal means by which chambers take on junior tenants, even a glowingly successful pupillage is no guarantee of a tenancy. Competition is intense. At the moment only about 60 per cent of those who make it to pupillage obtain tenancies. If you really are determined to make it as a barrister in private practice you may have to consider a third six. The important thing is not to lose heart.

Barristers in Scotland

A candidate for admission to the Faculty of Advocates is known as an 'intrant' and the Faculty publishes detailed *Regulations for Intrants*. An advocate is not only a member of the Faculty but also a member of the College of Justice and an officer of the Court. The procedure for admission of an intrant is subject in part to the control of the Faculty and in part to that of the Court. The first step, which is purely formal, is presentation of a petition to the Court via the clerk of the Faculty. The remit to the Faculty by the Court follows automatically and the prospective intrant may then proceed to matriculation. Before matriculating, the intrant must produce to the clerk of the Faculty a certificate of good character and provide references from two persons of standing in the community.

The period of professional training may, but need not be, undertaken before presentation of the petition. Prospective intrants are advised to enter into a training contract before they start their training so that they may, if they so wish, enter the solicitors' rather than the advocates' branch of the profession in due course.

Legal executives

Education, training and home-study schemes

Specialized education and training are needed to qualify as a legal executive. Most people study while they are working – by day release, evening classes or by taking a home-study correspondence course – combining study and examination with practical experience.

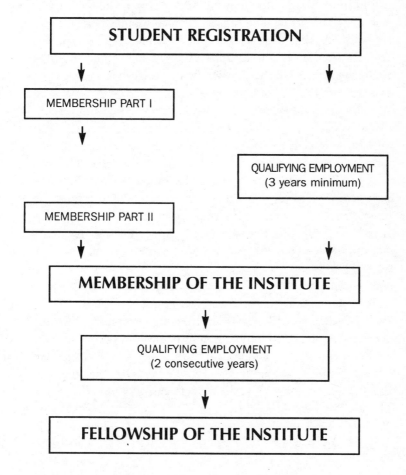

STUDENT REGISTRATION

MEMBERSHIP PART I

QUALIFYING EMPLOYMENT
(3 years minimum)

MEMBERSHIP PART II

MEMBERSHIP OF THE INSTITUTE

QUALIFYING EMPLOYMENT
(2 consecutive years)

FELLOWSHIP OF THE INSTITUTE

Qualifying as a legal executive
(*Source*: The Institute of Legal Executives)

The Institute of Legal Executives' (ILEX) training scheme leads to a professional qualification in law and legal practice. To start on the road to becoming a legal executive, check you have the qualifications needed (the ILEX Education Department will advise).

Enrolling as a student with the Institute

To enrol as a student with the Institute of Legal Executives you will need to have at least four GCSE passes at grades A, B or C. The subjects must include English language, English literature or English, and other passes must be drawn from a list of approved subjects provided by the Institute. Passes in only three approved GCSE subjects will be accepted, provided English is included and at least two of the subjects have been passed at A–level. The Institute may also accept other public examinations as evidence that a satisfactory educational level has been reached and, in the case of prospective mature students over the age of 25, the Institute may waive the basic educational requirement if it is considered that the individual has sufficient professional, business, commercial, academic or other experience. The Institute also now offers a Preliminary Certificate in Legal Studies, as an alternative to GCSEs, for those who cannot meet the minimum educational requirement, or who want some introductory legal studies.

There are three stages of qualification. Students commence their academic training by taking a series of courses which cover most of the areas of law and legal practice encountered in the legal profession. Although most students work in a legal environment while studying part-time, this is *not* a requirement. Students apply for enrolment into the Membership grade of ILEX on successful completion of Parts I and II of the Membership examination.

To achieve the full qualification of Fellow, Members of ILEX must be at least 25 years of age and have had five years' experience in a legal office (including at least two years after passing all the examinations).

Examinations

The Membership examination is set at two levels. Part I is usually taken over a period of two years. Four papers cover the English Legal System and essential elements of law and practice. The standard of these papers is comparable with GCE A level. Part II is usually taken over a period of two years. Four specialist papers must be passed, three in law and one in related legal practice. The Law papers are set at degree level. Exemptions may be granted from the examinations if a student has already passed other examinations of comparable standard and similar syllabus content, for example students with a recognized law degree are exempted from the law elements of the Part I and Part II membership examinations. Other qualifications in law at degree level or GCE A–level can give exemptions on a subject-for-subject basis.

You may also opt for a college course (they start in September every year) or a home-study course provided by ILEX Tutorial Services.

7 The future of the legal profession

One prediction that can safely be made is that the pattern of rapid – and sometimes painful – change which the legal profession has experienced in recent years will continue for the foreseeable future. Professor Richard Susskind, author of *The Future Of Law*, has argued that 'the legal marketplace will change beyond recognition as we progress into the information society'.

The impact of change will not be confined to any one area of the profession. A variety of factors explain the pressure for change – not just the widespread use and availability of sophisticated information technology, but also external pressures such as the government's attitude to legal aid funding and the need to satisfy clients who demand an ever-improving level of service. Certainly, the trend of recent years towards increasing specialization seems bound to continue.

The way in which change affects solicitors' firms will vary depending on the size and location of those firms. The major London practices are already international in nature. They look at the demand for legal services in a global context and are, for instance, alert to possible competition from major US law firms as well as from the major accountancy practices. Both in London and the provinces, there will continue to be mergers between medium-sized firms in an increasingly competitive market place. Already there are major national and regional firms and they will be keen to seek further growth, typically by swallowing firms with few resources or by 'cherry-picking' particular individuals or teams of lawyers from rival firms.

Small firms and sole practitioners will continue to be hard pressed. Professor Susskind believes that generalists will find their business squeezed most 'as many of their traditional domains become systematised and productised', but the future is not without hope for them, especially if they can develop a particular niche. Much will also depend on the Law Society's ability to promote the interests of its members while ensuring that client service throughout the UK continues to improve as well as on wider social, economic and political factors.

With the Bar, leading players should continue to prosper but the tendency for barristers to seek positions within firms of solicitors and accountants that demand advocacy skills may become more pronounced. The trend towards larger sets of chambers will continue as economies of scale are sought and clients demand greater specialization. As with solicitors' firms, there will in many quarters be a perception that small is not beautiful, since it may be easier to cope with change in an environment where a sophisticated infrastructure can be afforded.

The in-house lawyer will be less and less likely to act as a legal jack-of-all-trades. As the law becomes more complex, it will become common for even large in-house legal departments to outsource work to major private practices. Developing satisfactory relationships with those outside lawyers will be a key task. For lawyers working in central and local government, the future will, as always, depend to a large extent on the funding available.

In general, the future for legal support workers and those engaged in allied professions looks bright. Again, the effective use of information technology will be crucial. Opportunities for minority groups should increase as traditional barriers continue (however slowly) to crumble and part-time working and home working will almost inevitably become more common than at present.

8 Useful addresses

The Association of County Secretaries and Solicitors, The Secretary, Staffordshire County Council, County Building, Martin Street, Stafford ST16 6LH; 01785 223121

The Association of Law Costs Draftsmen, c/o Mrs S A Chapman, Church Cottage, Church Lane, Stuston, Diss, Norfolk IP21 4AG; 01379 741404

The Association for Shorthand Writers, c/o Margaret Wort, Edial Farm, Burntwood, Nr Walsall, Staffordshire

The Bar Association for Commerce, Finance and Industry, PO Box 366, Bracknell, Berkshire RG12 2FH; 01344 868752

The Bar Association for Local Government and Public Services, The Honorary Secretary, South Staffordshire District Council, Council Offices, Wolverhampton Road, Codsall, Wolverhampton WV8 1PX; 01204 522311

The Bar Council, Education and Training Department, 213 Cursitor Street, London EC4A 1NE; 0171 440 4000

British Institute of Verbatim Reports, 61 Carey Street, London WC2A 2JG. Contact: The Secretary, 73 Alicia Gardens, Kenton, Harrow, Middlesex HA3 8JD; 0181 907 8349

The Chartered Institute of Patent Agents, Staple Inn Buildings South, High Holborn, London WC1V 7PZ; 0171 405 9450

The Citizens' Advice Bureaux of Scotland, 26 George Square, Edinburgh EH8 9LD; 0131 667 0156

The Civil Service Commission. Contact Recruitment and Assessment Services Ltd, Innovation Centre, New Street, Basingstoke, Hampshire RG21 7DP; 01256 846466

The Civil Service Commission (Northern Ireland). Contact Recruitment Service, Department, Finance Personnel, Orchard House, 40 Foyle Street, Londonderry BT48 6AT; 01504 319900

The Council for Legal Education, Inns of Court, 4 Gray's Inn Place, London WC1R 5DX; 0171 404 5787

The Council for Licensed Conveyancers, 16 Glebe Road, Chelmsford, Essex, CM1 1QG; 01245 349599

Crown Prosecution Services, Recruitment Branch 2, 50 Ludgate Hill, London EC4M 7EX; 0171 273 8000

Director of Public Prosecutions for Northern Ireland, Royal Courts of Justice, 2 Chester Street, Belfast BT3 3NX; 01232 542444

Establishment Officer, Crown Office, 25 Chambers Street, Edinburgh EH1 1LD; 0131 226 2626⁻

The Faculty of Advocates, Advocates' Library, Parliament House,11 Parliament Square, Edinburgh EH1 1RF; 0131 226 5071

Faculty Services Ltd, Advocates' Library, Parliament House, 11 Parliament Square, Edinburgh EH1 1RF; 0131 226 5071

Government Legal Service Recruitment Team, Queen Anne's Chambers, 28 Broadway, London SW1H 90JS; 0171 210 3304

The Honourable Society of Middle Temple, The Students' Department, Middle Temple, London EC4Y 9AT; 0171 427 4800

The Institute of Barristers' Clerks, 4A Essex Court, London EC4Y 9AJ; 0171 353 2699

The Institute of Chartered Secretaries and Administrators, 16 Park Crescent, London W1N 4AH; 0171 580 4741

The Institute of Legal Executives, Kempston Manor, Kempston, Bedford, MK42 7AB; 01234 841000

The Institute of Paralegal Training, The Mill, Clymping, Littlehampton, West Sussex; 01903 714276

Law Centres Federation, Duchess House, 18–19 Warren Street, London W1P 1PL; 0171 387 8570

The Law Society, The Law Society's Hall, 113 Chancery Lane, London WC2A 1PL; 0171 242 1222

The Law Society's Careers and Recruitment Services, 227/228 Strand, London WC2R 1BA; 0171 242 1222

The Law Society's Legal Education Information Services, Ipsley Court, Berrington Close, Redditch, Worcestershire B98 OTD; 01527 504400

The Law Society of Northern Ireland, Law Society House, Victoria Street, 98–106 Victoria Street, Belfast BT1 3JZ; 011232 231614

The Law Society of Scotland, Legal Education Department, 26 Drumsheugh Gardens, Edinburgh EH3 7YR; 0131 226 7411

(You may also wish to check with your local Law Society. Its address can be found in your local telephone directory.)

The Lord Chancellor's Department, 54–60 Victoria Street, London SW1E 6QW; 0171 210 8500

LPC Central Applications Board, PO Box 84, Guildford, Surrey GU3 1YX; 01483 301282

National Association of Citizens' Advice Bureaux, 115–123 Pentonville Road, London N1 9LZ; 0171 833 2181

Northern Ireland Association of Citizens' Advice Bureaux, Regional Office, Newforge Lane, Belfast BT9 5NW; 01232 681117

Northern Ireland Court Service, Windsor House, 9–15 Bedford Street, Belfast BT2 7LT; 01232 328594

The Principal Chief Clerk and Clerk to the Committee of Magistrates for Inner London, Third Floor, North West Wing, Bush House, Aldwych, London WC2B 4PL; 0171 799 3332

Student Awards Agency for Scotland, Gyleview House, 3 Redheughs Rigg, South Gyle, Edinburgh EH12 9HH; 0131 244 5823

The Society of Public Notaries of London, Nigel Ready, c/o Cheesewrights, 10 Philpot Lane, London EC3M 8AA; 0171 623 9477

University Admission Services (UCAS), PO Box 28, Cheltenham,Gloucestershire Gl50 1HY; 01242 222444

Inns

The Honourable Society of Gray's Inn, The Education Department, 8 South Square, Gray's Inn, London WC1R 5EU; 0171 405 8164

The Honourable Society of Inner Temple, The Educational and Training Department, Inner Temple, London EC4Y 7HL; 0171 353 8462

The Honourable Society of the Inn of Court of Northern Ireland, The Royal Courts of Justice, Chichester Street, Belfast BT1 3JF; 01232 241523

The Honourable Society of Lincoln's Inn, The Students' Department,Treasury Office, Lincoln's Inn, London WC2A 3TL; 0171 405 1398

9 Further reading

General information

All the legal professional bodies produce their own pamphlets, which are available free of charge. These give details of qualification requirements and training and provide details of sources of further information.

The Law Society in London keeps a list of solicitors practising in England and Wales. The Society publishes useful careers booklets, including *Becoming a Solicitor* and *The Law Degree Route to Qualification as a Solicitor*. The latter sets out, among other matters details of institutions that offer qualifying law degrees and which are validated to run legal practice courses. In Scotland a list of solicitors is printed in the *Scottish Law Directory*, published by William Hodge & Co of 34–36 North Frederick Street, Glasgow, and in Northern Ireland the Law Society of Northern Ireland publishes an annual register of solicitors.

A list of all barristers practising in England and Wales can be found in the annual *Bar Directory* which is updated annually and published by ST Law and Tax, London. The Bar Council's booklet *Steps To The Bar* is free, send a sae and 52p for postage and packing to the Bar Council's Education and Training Department.

In England and Wales jobs for solicitors, legal executives, solicitors' clerks and law costs draftsmen in private practice, and vacancies in industry, government and commerce for solicitors, barristers, legal executives and solicitors' clerks are regularly advertised in: *The Times*, the *Guardian*, the *Independent*, the *Daily Telegraph*, the *Law Society's Gazette*, the *Guardian Gazette*, the *Solicitors' Journal*, the *New Law Journal*, the *Lawyer*, the *Local Government Chronicle*, the *Legal Action Group Bulletin*, and the *Legal Executive Journal*. In Scotland such jobs may be advertised in the *Scotsman*, the *Herald*, the *Journal of the Law Society of Scotland*, and the *Scots Law Times*. In Northern Ireland vacancies for lawyers may be found through advertisements in the *Belfast Telegraph*, the *Belfast Newsletter*, and the *Irish News*. Pupillage vacancies and details about available funding are listed in the annual Bar Council publication, the *Chambers, Pupillages and Awards Handbook*.

Further reading

Association of Graduate Careers Advisory Services, *The Legal Profession*, CSU Information Booklets.

Crown Office and Procurator Fiscal Service, *The Prosecution of Crime in Scotland*, Crown Office (1993). Available free of charge.

Dickson, Bruce, *The Legal System of Northern Ireland*, SLS Publications, (NI) (1984).

Du Cann, Richard, *The Art of the Advocate*, Penguin (1991).

Evans, Keith, *Advocacy at the Bar: A Beginner's Guide*, Financial Training Publications (1992).

MacQueen, Hector L, *Studying Scots Law*, Butterworths (1993).

Munkman, John, *The Technique of Advocacy*, Butterworths (1991).

Scottish Young Lawyers' Association, *A Law Degree – Then What?*, Scottish Young Lawyers' Association.

Susskind, Richard, *The Future of Law*, Oxford University Press (1996).

Walker, R J and Walker M G, *The English Legal System*, 6th edition, Butterworths (1985).

Williams, Glanville, *Learning the Law*, Stevens (1982).

Index

Northern Ireland, differences 4, 6, 23, 24,
    31, 33, 48, 50
    barristers 7, 21–2
    training 63, 69, 70
notaries 59–60

Open University 4
outdoor clerks 43–4

paralegals 24–7
partnerships 6, 11–12
patent agents 58–9
periodical advertisements 10, 88–9
practice managers 39–40
Practising Certificates 69
private practices 10–12, 18
Procurators Fiscal 23, 48
Professional Exams, Scotland 68
Professional Skills Course 66
prosecution services 48
pupillage 20, 74–8
Pupillage Applications Clearing House
    (PACH) 77–8
qualifications 62–81

Queen's Counsel (QC) 18

recruitment consultants 60–61
Register of Solicitors Employing Trainees
    (ROSET) 67

resident magistrates (RMs) 7
Roll of Solicitors 69, 70

salaried partnerships 11
salaries 4, 13, 51, 67, 71
Scotland, differences 3, 5, 24, 33, 44, 50,
    60
    advocates 6–7, 15, 18–19, 21
    advocates' clerks 30–31
    Procurators Fiscal 23, 48
    training 63, 68–9, 78
scrivener notaries 59–60
self–employment 17
Senior Counsel 18
shorthand writers 31–33
'silks' 18
'sixes' 75–6
size of firms 12–13
solicitors 5–7, 9–15, 63–73, 82–3
specialization 4, 13, 16, 19
stipendiary magistrates 7, 49

'taxation' proceedings 35
teachers 56–7
temporary work 41–42
'tenancies' 20, 78
training 62–81
training contracts 66–7

women 4, 7–8